Developing Open Access Journals

Developing Open Access Journals: A practical guide

DAVID SOLOMON

Chandos Publishing

Oxford · England

Chandos Publishing (Oxford) Limited
TBAC Business Centre
Avenue 4
Station Lane
Witney
Oxford OX28 4BN
UK
Tel: +44 (0) 1993 848726 Fax: +44 (0) 1865 884448
E-mail: info@chandospublishing.com
www.chandospublishing.com

First published in Great Britain in 2008

ISBN:
978 1 84334 339 4 (paperback)
978 1 84334 340 0 (hardback)
1 84334 339 8 (paperback)
1 84334 340 1 (hardback)

British Library Cataloguing-in-Publication Data.
A catalogue record for this book is available from the British Library.

Typeset by Domex e-Data Pvt. Ltd.
Printed in the UK and USA.

Contents

List of tables

About the author

David J. Solomon is a professor in the Department of Medicine at Michigan State University's College of Human Medicine and holds a joint appointment in the Office of Medical Education Research and Development. He received his doctoral degree in 1981 from Michigan State University in educational psychology, specializing in measurement and evaluation. He has worked in medical education for 19 years, at both Michigan State University and the University of Texas Medical Branch in Galveston, Texas (UTMB). He has been involved in research and development on a variety of projects in performance assessment, primary care education, curriculum development and distance learning, mainly in undergraduate and graduate internal medicine educational programs.

In 1996, while a faculty member at UTMB, Dr Solomon started an open access journal in medical education, *Medical Education Online (MEO)*, with the help of colleagues in the Office of Educational Development. *MEO* has become a well-established international journal and is currently co-edited by Dr Solomon and Dr Ann Frye, the director of the Office of Educational Development. Dr Solomon has written extensively about open access publishing, and his experiences in developing and editing *MEO* form much of the basis of this book.

Dr Solomon lives with his wife in Haslett, Michigan, near where he was born, and has two grown sons. He can be contacted at:

A-202 E Fee Hall
Michigan State University
E. Lansing MI, 48824 USA
E-mail: dsolomon@msu.edu
Tel: 011 517 353 2037 Ext 223

List of acronyms

APA	American Psychological Association
BMC	BioMed Central
CSS	cascading style sheets
DOAJ	Directory of Open Access Journals
ERIC	Educational Resources Information Center
FTP	file transfer protocol
HTML	hypertext markup language
ICMJE	International Committee of Medical Journal Editors
INSPEC	Engineering Village, Library, Information Science & Technology Abstracts
IP	internet protocol
IRB	institutional review board
ISSN	International Standard Serial Number
LISA	Library and Information Science Abstracts
LOCKSS	lots of copies keeps stuff safe
OA	open access
OAI	open access initiative
ODP	Open Directory Project
OJS	Open Journal System
PDF	portable document format
PKP	Public Knowledge Project
PLoS	Public Library of Science
SciELO	Scientific Electronic Library Online
SEO	search engine optimization
STM	scientific, technical and medical

URL	uniform resource locator
USB	universal serial bus
XML	extendable markup language

Part I
Background information

Introduction

Scholarly journals have been distributed over electronic networks for more than 25 years (Parang and Saunders, 1994). The early journals were text-based, however, and did not provide a practical alternative to traditional paper distribution of journals. With the public release of the World Wide Web in 1993, electronic distribution of journals became practical, and within ten years, by at least one measure, became the dominant means of distributing scholarly journals (Van Orsdel and Born, 2002). The dramatic differences between paper and electronic distribution have opened an array of new possibilities as well as creating a number of challenges for our scholarly journal system. Although there are now thousands of journals distributed electronically, the system continues to evolve and we still have much to learn about how to make the best use of this new medium.

One of the most striking differences between paper and electronic publication is the cost of distribution. For paper journals, the cost of distributing each copy is significant and the only practical means of funding these journals is through subscription fees. With electronic distribution, the cost of dissemination disappears, making it possible to distribute journals freely to anyone who wants to access them and find other means of funding the operation of the journal. Calls for distributing journals at no cost and finding other means of funding began almost as soon as journals appeared in electronic formats, and have developed into what is known as the open access initiative (OAI). The ethical and practical advantages of open access (OA) have been widely discussed (Harnad, 2003; Willinsky, 2006).

Although costs remain, electronic distribution and other advances in computer technology have significantly reduced the resources required to publish scholarly journals. Prior to modern computer and networking technology, only large organizations had the resources to publish journals. Today it is quite possible for small groups of scholars and even single individuals to create and maintain high-quality peer-reviewed electronic journals. Since the development of the web, thousands of OA electronic journals have been developed without the resources of traditional publishers. While many have quickly vanished, others have grown to become respected and widely read. Despite misconceptions to the contrary, most of these journals manage to operate without charging readers for access to their contents or authors for publication (Kaufman-Will Group, 2005). They operate on volunteer effort and small subsidies from a variety of sources, and are becoming a growing means of disseminating scholarship.

Although developing and operating OA journals is well within the means of a small group of colleagues, such as societal special-interest groups or university departments, it takes specialized knowledge from a range of fields that is not readily available to most university faculty members. There are also a variety of ways these journals can be structured and operated. The goal of this book is to provide a guide to developing and operating an OA journal that covers what is needed to develop a successful OA journal, along with examples and advice on issues to consider in deciding how to structure and operate a newly formed OA journal.

Structure of the book

This book is designed to be a very practical guide on developing OA journals. It is largely based on my experience developing and operating an OA journal in medical education, *Medical Education Online* (*MEO*). It also reflects my biases and experience in developing *MEO*. To try to counter these biases and give readers an idea of the range of options for designing a new journal, four other successful OA journals with a variety of different structures and formats are described in Chapter 2. These journals are used throughout the book as examples of approaches for organizing and operating an OA journal.

The book is divided into three parts. The first, which includes the rest of this chapter and the next, contains background information that I believe will be useful for someone starting a new scholarly journal. This includes a brief history of scholarly journals, a discussion of the various purposes scholarly journals serve, some of the practical and ethical arguments for making scholarship freely accessible and a category scheme for OA journals based on how they are funded. Chapter 2 provides a description of the five OA journals that, as noted above, will serve throughout the book as examples of various ways of implementing an OA journal.

The second part of the book concentrates on the process of designing, setting up and implementing an OA journal. The third chapter focuses on planning for a new journal, and addresses issues such as defining the scope, developing a peer-review policy and process, editorial board structure and membership, and defining the journal format and sections. Chapter 4 covers web hosting and data management issues, including the choice of a journal management system, web hosting options and security. The fifth chapter discusses developing journal policies on matters such as copyright and intellectual property, addressing complaints, submission policies, conflict of interest and, if appropriate, addressing the protection of human subjects in research. Chapter 6 covers obtaining resources for operating the journal, including potential sources of funding, strategies for operating an OA journal efficiently and the use and promotion of volunteerism in operating OA journals. Chapter 7 focuses on options for indexing and archiving the journal's content to increase visibility and accessibility and ensure the long-term survival of the material contained in the journal.

The third part of the book focuses on operating and maintaining an OA journal. Chapter 8 covers strategies for launching and publicizing a new OA journal. The ninth chapter addresses issues in maintaining and sustaining OA journals over time, including managing the review process, working with authors to complete revisions, copy-editing and typesetting, website maintenance and strategies for sustainability. The last chapter covers other sources of information on OA journals.

A brief history of scholarly journals

Peer-reviewed scholarly journals first appeared around 340 years ago. Prior to the development of these journals, scientific communication in Europe had been largely conducted via letters between scientists that were often copied and sent out to multiple other scientists, and then frequently further distributed by reading the contents of the letters at local meetings of scientists (Meadows, 1980). The system was obviously far from ideal: along with being inefficient, it tended to obscure the origins of the information, which often let to friction over who deserved the credit for new ideas and findings.

Although there is some controversy over which was the first scholarly journal, most historians agree that the *Philosophical Transactions of the Royal Society of London*, first published in 1665, was the first journal of the type we would recognize as a peer-reviewed scholarly journal whose contents largely include original research and scholarship described by the scientists or scholars who conducted the research or scholarship (Kronick, 1976). A French journal had appeared a few months earlier than *Philosophical Transactions*: *Le Journal des Sçavans* was founded by Denis de Lallo de la Courdraye and is often considered to be the first scientific journal. However, *Le Journal des Sçavans* had a much broader scope than just publishing original research, and, according to Guédon (2001), was probably closer in format to a journal like *Scientific America*.

Philosophical Transactions was conceived by Henry Oldenburg, who was the secretary of the Royal Society of London at the time. Prior to developing the journal, Oldenburg's office was a major distribution point for scientific letters. The effort to fulfill this role may have be part of what motivated Oldenburg to develop *Philosophical Transactions* (Meadows, 1980). According to Guédon (2001), Oldenburg's other major impetus for starting the journal was to address controversy over the origin and ownership of the intellectual property contained in these letters. The journal was able to act almost like a 'patent office' for ideas, establishing paternity for a scientist's theories and findings. Through publication in *Philosophical Transactions*, scientists (or, as they were called at the time, natural philosophers) were able to assert ownership of their work while allowing them to disseminate their ideas and findings. In addition, through peer review, the journal not only bestowed legitimacy to claims of ownership for ideas and discoveries but also a seal of merit for a natural philosopher's work. The genius of Oldenburg's creation was not lost on his contemporaries: other scientific societies, which were appearing throughout Europe at this time, began creating their own journals.

Over the next 300 years many of the key features of these journals remained largely unchanged. These scholarly journals were almost exclusively owned and operated by scientific societies for the benefit of the societies and their members. The journals mainly published original research and scholarship authored by the scientist who conducted the research or scholarship. They were expensive to publish, but the societies and their members were willing to take on the financial burden of operating the journals because they were valuable.

This state of affairs continued up until after the Second World War. During the 1950s and 1960s, governments, particularly in the USA but throughout the developed world, began investing heavily in basic scientific research, mainly through their university systems. As the research enterprise grew, the research libraries within these universities also grew, along with the need for journal space as this huge investment in research began to bear fruit. Not only was the amount of research and ensuing journal publications growing but, as the knowledge base expanded, whole new fields of research began evolving. The net result was a growing need for both increased journal space and new journals to cover the expanding and different fields in science and technology. While the rise of the research university system has impacted on all scholarly journals, the effects were far more noticeable in what librarians have termed the scientific, technical and medical (STM) journals.

At this time starting a new journal was a very expensive undertaking. The scholarly societies, which up until this point had almost exclusively published these journals, could not keep up with the need for both increased journal space and the development of new journals to cover evolving scientific disciplines. The commercial publishers – which had largely avoided owning scientific journals, since they were at best a break-even and usually a money-losing enterprise – began to test the waters of scientific publishing. While in the past publishing scientific journals was not particularly profitable, publishers found they could make money in this new era of increased government funding of scientific research; in fact, ironically, lots of money! What ensued over the period between about 1970 and the present has been called by librarians the 'serial-pricing crisis'. Over this period the price of serials (journals) began rising at well ahead of the general inflation rate. Initially the entry of commercial publishers into scholarly publishing was probably beneficial, filling a real need for more journals and journal space. But by the mid-1990s the rising cost of STM journals began to limit the ability of libraries to maintain their collections (Association of Research Libraries, 2004).

It seems quite clear the root cause of the serial-pricing crisis has been the lack of free-market forces controlling subscription fees, particularly for STM journals. This assertion is supported by the huge differences in the cost per character of information published in different scientific and scholarly fields and between commercial and non-profit publishers within the same field (Bergstrom, 2002). Guédon (2001) has largely attributed the serial crisis to the impact of the Scientific Citation Index, which he believes is responsible for the development of 'core journals'. These journals are so central to their discipline that librarians have little choice but to purchase subscriptions to them, whatever the cost, or suffer a revolt among the faculty at their institution. Though it is probably true that the Scientific Citation Index, by quantifying journal 'impact', had an effect, I suspect the tacit understanding among scholars of which are the key journals in their field would have created much the same result. In any event, many commercial publishers and a few societies were quick to take advantage of the opportunity to raise the library subscription fees for their journals through the roof. In addition, the opportunity for commercial publishers to make huge profits from scientific publishing resulted in a rush both to create new journals and to buy up as many existing journals as possible. This has resulted in a rapid consolidation of the commercial publishing industry. Reed Elsevier, the largest scientific publisher, alone acquired over 400 journals in 2000 (Willinsky and Wolfson, 2001). By the beginning of the 21st century, the landscape of scholarly publishing had been completely changed. Today, commercial publishers own 45 per cent of scholarly journals and assist in publishing an additional 17 per cent of these journals for societies. In the STM market, a mere seven commercial publishers own around 30 per cent of the journals, accounting for over 60 per cent of the total revenue in that highly profitable market (Crow, 2006).

By the mid-1990s electronic dissemination of journals became feasible, and threw the whole scholarly publishing system into turmoil. With electronic publication, many of the roles that librarians and publishers have played in maintaining the journal system have begun to disappear. Additionally, it is not clear who will fulfill the roles that remain. On one hand, librarians could become little more than specialized purchasing agents who buy large blocks of content from massive commercial publishers that distribute material directly from their own servers to readers. The major publishers are clearly positioning to try to make this the dominant scholarly publishing model. On the other hand, a growing number of people are asking just what benefits the publishers provide, and are these benefits worth the price that is being charged for journal subscriptions? In addition, there is growing worldwide support for the open access initiative, and this is beginning to result in legislation requiring at least some type of open access to publicly funded research and scholarship.

With electronic publication we are no longer limited to a single publishing model, and it appears that at least for the foreseeable future a variety of different publishing models will operate in parallel. While still accounting for only a fraction of the overall scholarly publishing system, there are currently in excess of 2,700 OA journals in the Directory of Open Access Journals (DOAJ). OA journals operated by small groups of colleagues will never be the dominant form of scholarly publishing; but at the same time their numbers continue to grow, as does the quality of the material they contain and their acceptance among scholars.

The functions of journals in scholarly communities

When developing a new scholarly journal, it is useful to keep in perspective the roles journals play in scientific and scholarly communities. Ann Schafner (1994) outlined five distinct though overlapping roles played by these journals in scholarly communities. While one could probably 'cut the pie' in different ways, I have found her conception of these roles extremely helpful.

Building a collective knowledge base

Probably the most important role journals play is forming our archive of knowledge. Most would agree these journals form the most comprehensive, up-to-date and authoritative archive of information in a given scholarly field. Obviously, the accuracy and quality of the material contained in this archive is of central importance. Peer review serves as one of the most important mechanisms for validating the information contained in these journals.

It generally takes about 18 months from submission for a peer-reviewed article to be published. This can be reduced to some extent by web-based peer review and electronic publication; however, the peer-review and revision process just takes time. Also, the care and effort it takes to develop a publishable manuscript means it can be months between the date research is conducted and the date results are even submitted for publication. Additionally, manuscripts are often not accepted the first time they are submitted to a journal, and may be resubmitted to several journals before being accepted for publication. The net result is that the information disseminated through peer-reviewed journals is often several years old.

From the perspective of our archive of knowledge, the speed with which the archive is updated, while not trivial, is far less of a concern than accuracy and the quality of the material contained in these journals. I think most scholars would agree that getting it right through the care and effort of peer review and careful revision, copy-editing and typesetting far outweighs the need for rapid publication in the process of forming an archive of knowledge.

Communicating information

Communication among scholars working in the same field seems a similar and somewhat overlapping role to the one above. It is, however, qualitatively quite different from forming an archive of knowledge. Speed and interactivity are much more important in this role. At the same time, peer review is far less important, as experts in a field are perfectly capable of making their own decisions about the value and accuracy of the information that is being disseminated.

Journals probably played a much more central role in this type of communication early in their history. With other more efficient means of communication available today, one would think journals would have a very limited role in communicating research results among scholars working in a particular field. It is not clear that this is the case. First, the research on informal communication of science and engineering knowledge suggests the modes of communication vary substantially among fields. For example, pre-print archives such as arXiv.org were quickly embraced by a number of fields, but are rarely used in other fields despite concerted attempts to implement them (speaking from my own experience in educational research). The research on informal communication among scientists also suggests, ironically, that much of what is discussed turns out to be journal articles (Schafner, 1994). While pre-print archives, listservs and threaded discussions are likely to grow in importance for communicating new science and scholarship, journals clearly retain a significant role in communication among scholars working in a particular field.

Validating the quality of research

Journals play an important role in maintaining community standards on how research and scholarship are conducted. To some extent this is implemented by acting as a filtering mechanism in what is published and hence disseminated. The effects can also be subtler. The work of experienced scholars rarely receives harsh reviews. That is not to say they always get their manuscripts published, but they tend to have internalized the norms of the field and know how the research or scholarship should be conducted and described, and are much less likely than novices to be chastised by reviewers. There is not universal agreement that this is entirely a good thing. Some have argued it stifles creativity and unnecessarily subjects novice researchers to harsh criticism (Kumashiro, 2005). More importantly, it can inhibit the dissemination of novel ideas that may turn out to be major advancements in science. Whether good or bad, journals clearly play a role in maintaining norms for the way research and scholarship are conducted in a field.

Distributing rewards

Publication in peer-reviewed journals is one of the major ways scholars are evaluated. Not only is quantity important, but which journals one publishes in is general equally if not more important. As noted, the roots of this role of peer-reviewed journals go all the way back to the formation of *Philosophical Transactions of the Royal Society of London* in the middle of the 17th century. While tenure decisions were not involved, an important function of the journal was establishing who deserved credit for specific findings or theories. This role clearly has expanded as a more general measure of achievement as a scholar.

Building scientific communities

Not all the information in scholarly journals strictly focuses on scholarship. These journals also act as a means of tying a scholarly community together in a number of ways. A hallmark of a new discipline's coming of age is the establishment of a new journal – in essence, staking out the intellectual territory of the new field. Beyond that, editorials, opinion articles and letters to the editor often serve as a forum to debate the current issues in the discipline. Sometimes they are substantive and sometimes they extend to related areas, such as the social implications of findings, funding and/or training issues within the field. Journals also commonly serve as a forum for news such as appointments to major positions or the passing of a well-known member of the community. While this role may be diminishing to some extent with the variety of communication options available to scholars, journals continue to play an important role in forming and maintaining scholarly communities.

Ethical and practical arguments for open access to scholarship

With the conversion from paper to electronic distribution it has become possible to disseminate scholarly journals at no cost and find other means of funding the resources necessary to publish them. This section will cover some of the practical and ethical arguments for moving to an open access model for scholarly journals.

Scholarly articles are a unique form of intellectual property. The creators generally are not interested in profiting directly from the distribution of their material. As noted in the previous section, publishing scholarly journal articles rewards their authors in the form of recognition, promotion, career advancement and enhancing the likelihood of receiving grants for future research and scholarship. These indirect rewards are all that scholars seek in return for making their articles public. It is also clearly in their best interest to have their articles distributed as widely as possible. Not only does it seem intuitively obvious that open access would increase the dissemination, but there is now a growing body of empirical evidence confirming this (OpCit Project, 2006).

Open access also makes science and scholarship operate more efficiently. Journals serve an important role in the communication of research, and scientists and scholars generally consult dozens of journal articles in conducting or reporting the results of a research study. Prior to the development of web-based journals, accessing the literature meant many hours in the library locating and copying relevant articles. While it varies from field to field, most serial publications are now available 24 hours a day, seven days a week, from any internet-enabled computer, and the time it takes to access and print them is a fraction of what it takes to access them in paper form at a library. While this is true for both OA and fee-for-access journals, OA journals can be accessed much more efficiently than fee-for-access journals. Accessing an OA journal article simply involves 'clicking' on a hyperlink, generally directly from where the reference was located. While most scholars in the developed world can access much of the fee-for-access literature through the electronic holdings of their university libraries, it is much more complicated and time-consuming to access the material. It generally involves working through one's library electronic journal portal to the publisher's website, and locating the specific journal, volume, issue and finally the article itself before it can be downloaded. In my experience, this tends to be a frustrating five-minute process compared with a single 'click' of a link to access an OA journal article. As scholars generally review dozens of articles in the course of conducting a study or writing a journal paper, the added effort of accessing fee-for-access journals wastes a significant amount of time.

Although scientists and scholars in the developed world generally have reasonably good access to most of the fee-for-access published literature through their libraries, those in the developing world do not. Their libraries cannot afford to pay the library subscription fees charged by publishers – particularly for the STM journals, whose fees are often exorbitant. The situation has improved, since many publishers are now providing libraries in developing countries with free or reduced-price access to their electronic holdings, but scientists and scholars in developing countries still have limited access to the fee-for-access literature. The fact they do not have good access to this literature hurts us all, by limiting the ability of these scholars to participate in the exchange of information. Not only does this reduce the aggregate brain-power working on many of the pressing problems the world faces, but in significant areas of research the scientists of the developing world are in a better position to address key problems. A good example is the epidemiology of developing epidemics.

Beyond the practical issues cited above, there are strong ethical imperatives for making the scientific and scholarly literature freely available and finding other ways of funding publication. Willinsky (2006) has called the knowledge gained from scientific and scholarly study 'public knowledge', since it is largely funded from public sources. Willinsky argues convincingly that the knowledge resulting from this research and scholarship belongs to the public who funded the research, and should be made freely available. This argument has been gaining increasing popularity, and more and more governments are moving to require researchers to make at least the 'pre-prints' of their published manuscripts freely available through public archives.

Prior to electronic dissemination becoming feasible, the only practical means of funding the cost of scholarly journals was through charging for each copy distributed. In a span of less than 15 years electronic dissemination has taken over as the predominant means by which peer-reviewed journals are distributed, and charging for access as a means of funding these journals simply no longer makes sense. At the same time, the huge scholarly publishing system will not change quickly. There is tremendous inertia, not to mention a vested interest in keeping one of the most profitable sectors of the world economy in business. Despite these forces, the transition to open access journals seems to be speeding up and evolving into a variety of different models, which will be discussed in the next section.

Models for open access publication

As we will see from the journals that will be used as examples in Chapter 2, OA journals can be implemented in a number of ways. At the most basic level there are two strategies for providing open access to scholarship, which are often termed the 'green' and 'gold' roads to open access. The green road refers to creating open access repositories for articles that were either previously published in a fee-for-access journal (post-prints) or the version of the article prior to it being published in a fee-for-access journal (pre-prints). The gold road is the development of open access journals. There is some controversy over which model should be pursued. My personal biases are obvious, but both strategies are valuable and I believe it is a mistake to waste effort arguing over which is the best. As long as the manuscripts are adequately indexed so they can be found and sufficiently archived so there is some confidence they will be accessible for the foreseeable future, both roads take us where we need to go.

Willinsky (2006: 212–13) provides a useful framework for categorizing OA journals, largely based on how they are funded. The scheme below is a slightly modified version of Willinsky's scheme.

- *Author fee.* The journal is funded by charges to the authors. Generally authors are only charged for published articles, though some journals charge a processing fee for submissions.

- *Subsidized.* The costs of operating the journal are subsidized from some source or a number of sources. One of the most common sources is volunteer labor from a small group of people who operate the journal, but libraries, university departments and governmental agencies are other common sources of support.

- *Added value.* Providing an OA version of articles, usually in HTML, and charging for higher-quality versions, possibly in PDF format or print, to generate revenue to cover the costs of operating the journal.

- *Delayed.* Charging for immediate access to articles to cover the costs of the journal, and at some later time making the articles open access.

- *Partial.* Only a (usually small) number of the articles are made freely available. The rest are fee-for-access.

- *Selected.* The material is freely available to certain groups of people, while only available to others for a fee. Usually used to provide access for scholars in developing countries.

- *Cooperative.* Multiple journals are published cooperatively, sharing resources such as web hosting, copy-editing and journal management software and taking advantage of economies of scale. Usually funded through subsidies.

My strong personal preference is for finding a source of funding for subsidizing the costs associated with publishing. Implementing a cooperative model where multiple OA journals share resources is a great way to reduce costs through economies of scale. Throughout this book strategies for operating a journal efficiently and minimizing costs will be discussed; however, there is no way around the fact that publishing a peer-reviewed journal, even on the internet, requires resources.

The delayed, partial and restricted models all limit access to the material that is published. While a clear improvement over fee-for-access, these models are less than ideal. The author-fee model also has serious disadvantages. Many publishers, such as BioMed Central, that employ this model have mechanisms to waive fees for scholars from developing countries and/or authors without the ability to pay. This addresses the most obvious problem with this model, but not all the problems. I believe the model still tends to discourage at least some authors from publishing in these journals – although in fairness, publishers like BioMed Central and the Public Library of Science (PLoS) have managed to be quite successful in attracting submissions.

Charging for added-value versions and the somewhat related option of generating income from advertising on the journal website are attractive strategies that have the potential of generating a revenue stream for publishing OA journals while making all their content freely available. Unfortunately I suspect these strategies can only generate a significant amount of funding for very successful OA journals, and since the amount of resources needed to operate a journal go up with success, these strategies may not generate adequate resources for operating even very successful OA journals.

While finding a means of subsidizing an OA journal is challenging, I believe this strategy offers the best overall option for implementing OA journals. For new OA journals formed by a small society, special-interest group, department or a group of colleagues, the resources required can initially be very modest and involve almost if not entirely volunteer effort. For more ambitious efforts, and for when these journals become successful, other options exist. Strategies for minimizing costs, operating an OA journal efficiently and securing resources are discussed in more detail in Chapter 6.

In the next chapter we will review five successful OA journals and how they have addressed obtaining resources and implementing the various aspects of operating an OA journal. These journals will be used as examples throughout the rest of the book.

2

Examples of successful open access journals

This chapter presents five well-established and successful open access journals. Each of the journals is quite different, and they were chosen to provide examples of the variety of approaches one can take to addressing the various aspects of creating and operating an OA journal. The chapter provides a brief overview of each journal: its history, scope, financing, review procedures, policies, governance, archiving/indexing and publication formats.[1] The chapter ends with a summary contrasting the similarities and differences among the journals. Throughout the rest of the book, I will use these journals as examples as we discuss in more depth how one might address designing and operating an OA journal.

Medical Education Online

History

Medical Education Online (www.med-ed-online.org) was founded by the author as a web portal designed to facilitate communication concerning educating physicians and other health professionals. The site initially contained a variety of content, including a peer-reviewed journal, sections for resources and posting informational notices and a threaded discussion list. Most of these sections were later dropped because it was felt that there were better alternatives available or other modes of electronic communication that were a better vehicle for that type of communication. The peer-reviewed journal, which was always the central focus of *MEO*, has grown into a well-established OA journal.

MEO was launched in April 1996 with several invited articles. For the first five years the journal received between ten and 20 submissions a year, and published around six or eight of these manuscripts. After the journal had been established, the workload during this period was moderate and I maintained the journal by myself. But around 2000 the submissions to the journal began steadily increasing. In 2005 the journal went through an editorial board change and, due to a number of unrelated events, fell several months behind in processing manuscript submissions. In 2006 an electronic submissions process was implemented and the journal began using a distributed review procedure with several review editors and two managing editors. The new system has worked extremely well and we no longer have a backlog of submissions. In 2006 the journal received 100 submissions and published 32 articles. It is accessed each month by approximately 17,000 unique IP addresses from over 100 countries.

Scope

The journal includes articles on any aspect of the process of training health professionals. Despite this rather broad scope, approximately 10 per cent of the submissions we receive are outside the range of the journal – often articles focusing on clinical medicine.

Financial

Up until recently *MEO* operated entirely on volunteer effort. The journal had no budget and the only cost had been to secure the website and domain name from a commercial internet service provider. In April 2007 the journal began hosting advertisements, with the hope of generating enough income to cover the costs of professional copy-editing and conversion of articles to XML (extendable markup language). To date this advertising has only been generating around US$100 per month, which is not adequate to cover these costs.

Review process

Since 2006 *MEO* has used a two-stage review process that relies on two managing editors and six review editors. *MEO* also uses highly automated web-based submission and review management software that I developed using open source software. One of the managing editors initially reviews each submission. If the manuscript is not within the scope of the journal or is clearly not publishable, the author is informed and the manuscript is rejected. Otherwise, the submission is assigned to one of the review editors who manage the peer-review and revision process. A little under half of the manuscripts received are sent out for peer review, and the majority of these are published with revisions. Our goal is for the review process to be completed within four to six weeks, although in many cases we have not been able to achieve this target.

Rights management and editorial policies

The journal policies are available at www.med-ed-online.org/policy.htm. As part of the submission process, authors affirm their acceptance of a publication agreement (www.med-ed-online.org/agreement.htm) which gives the journal a limited license to publish but allows the authors to retain copyright to their material. I hold the copyright to the journal name, structure and organization. The journal also has a complaints policy and policies requiring appropriate review of human subject research and disclosure of conflicts of interest.

Governance

The editorial board comprises two managing editors, six review editors and a librarian, who helps with copy-editing, reference checking and the development of plans for indexing and archiving. The journal also had a graduate student working on an internship. The managing editors handle day-to-day decisions and consult the rest of the editorial board on major policy issues. At the present time there are no by-laws or other written documents outlining formal governance procedures for the journal. Since *MEO* has had no specific operating budget until recently, we have not applied for non-profit tax status.

Indexing and archiving

MEO is indexed by PsycINFO and archived through the LOCKSS system. We believe the journal will be accepted for inclusion in PubMed Central, but have not had the resources to meet the requirement to convert manuscripts into an acceptable XML format. Additionally we have applied for and are waiting word on the journal's acceptance into the Educational Resources Information Center (ERIC).

Structure, content and formatting

Three general types of articles are solicited. Feature articles discuss issues of general interest to the health education community – for example, presenting perspectives as well as reviews and commentary on the literature on a specific topic. Research articles present high-quality completed research or evaluation studies. Trend articles present new ideas as well as studies or descriptions of programs in the early stages of development. All articles are peer reviewed by between two and six external consultants. The journal also publishes letters to the editor and occasional book reviews, all of which are reviewed by one of the managing editors.

MEO is organized into yearly volumes and publishes articles within volumes as they become ready for publication. New articles are announced via a free subscription service to about 800 subscribers and via DR-ED, a widely read listserv in medical education.

MEO originally published manuscripts in both HTML and PDF formats. During the first few years of operation the majority of readers accessed the HTML version; but over time there was a shift to the majority accessing the PDF version, so in 2005 the HTML version was dropped.

Information Research

History

Information Research (http://informationr.net/ir/index.html) was first published in April 1995 as an electronic version of a print journal, *Information Research News,* that published papers by faculty and students at the University of Sheffield's Department of Information Studies. It quickly evolved into a fully refereed international journal publishing articles and working papers that include the results of research across a wide range of information-related disciplines. It is privately published by Professor T.D. Wilson, Professor Emeritus at the University of Sheffield, with support from Lund University Libraries, Lund, Sweden and the Swedish School of Library and Information Science at Högskolan i Borås.

Scope

IR publishes both refereed papers and working papers in the fields of information science, information management, information systems, information policy and librarianship, although in recent years the number of working papers has declined. The journal also publishes book and software reviews, conference proceedings, other special articles and a short editorial in each issue.

Financial

IR relies largely on the volunteer effort of the editor/publisher, Professor Wilson, but does receive technical support from Lund University Libraries and editorial support from the Swedish School of Library and Information Science at Gothenburg University and Högskolan i Borås. The journal is also seeking to generate income through indexing and content services, and by operating as an 'Amazon Associate' with links from book reviews to the book in Amazon.com as a means of generating some income. *IR* is willing to accept advertisements as logos on pages of the journal.

Review process

Papers are first reviewed by the editor; if considered to be within the scope of the journal, they are then circulated to two referees, selected for their expertise in the area of the submitted paper. Members of the editorial board also act as referees where appropriate. The majority of papers submitted usually require revision before publication – overall, the acceptance rate of the journal is approximately 35 per cent of submitted papers. The review process is rapid and articles submitted at the beginning of a quarter are usually published in the next quarterly issue.

Rights management and editorial policies

Information Research is a free electronic journal whose aim is to encourage the free exchange of the results of scholarly research for the benefit of the various communities of interest within the information professions. To this end, authors retain copyright to their articles and make them available under the terms of a Creative Commons license. The terms of the license are as follows.

- *Attribution.* The licensor permits others to copy, distribute, display and perform the work. In return, licensees must give the original author credit.

- *Non-commercial.* The licensor permits others to copy, distribute, display and perform the work. In return, licensees may not use the work for commercial purposes – unless they get the licensor's permission.

- *No derivative works.* The licensor permits others to copy, distribute, display and perform only unaltered copies of the work – not derivative works based on it.

In submitting to *Information Research*, authors agree to the publisher licensing the content to appropriate search engines and database providers to ensure maximum exposure of the content to the intended audiences, on the understanding that any income received by the journal is used only to support its development and publication.

Persons or publishers wishing to download a paper for whatever use (other than personal study) must contact the author for permission. However, in submitting to *Information Research*, authors agree to their paper being published under the terms set out above. Copyright for the editorials, author and subject indexes and the design of the journal is held by the publisher, Professor Wilson.

Indexing and archiving

The journal is indexed through Google Scholar, INSPEC, LISA, Social Science Citation Index, Current Contents/Social and Behavioral Sciences, ISI Alerting Services, Social Scisearch and Journal Citation Reports/Social Sciences Edition. *IR* is listed in the catalogues and directories of resources of several hundred university and college libraries around the world, and in the major internet search tools such as the Yahoo! directory.

Structure, content and formatting

The journal is organized into yearly volumes with quarterly issues, and published in XHTML. To facilitate formatting, an XHTML template is provided to prospective authors along with some guidance in creating the draft manuscript. Manuscripts are generally published in English, although some material is published in Spanish.

Journal of Medical Internet Research

History

The *Journal of Medical Internet Research* (www.jmir.org/) editorial board was assembled in 1998 and the first articles were published in August 1999. The *JMIR* was conceived and founded by Gunther Eysenbach, MD, MPH, who continues as editor and publisher. It was the first international scientific peer-reviewed journal covering all aspects of research, information and communication in healthcare using internet- and intranet-related technologies. As the journal is about the internet, the editors are also dedicated to using and experimenting with the internet as a communication vehicle. The *JMIR* has grown to be a very widely read journal accessed by approximately 27,000 unique IP addresses a month; approximately 16,000 readers subscribe to e-mail notices of publication (all as of January 2007).

Scope

The *JMIR* publishes manuscripts on all aspects of research, information and communication in the healthcare field using internet and other e-health technologies. This field overlaps with what is called 'consumer health informatics'. The journal also publishes original research on development, evaluation and application of other (non-internet) e-technologies in the healthcare setting. The *JMIR* targets a broad readership consisting of health professionals, policy-makers, consumers, health informaticians, developers, researchers, hospital and healthcare administrators and e-health businesses.

As e-health is a highly interdisciplinary field, the *JMIR* invites research papers from a range of disciples, including the medical sciences, the computer, behavioral, social and communication sciences, psychology, library sciences, informatics, human-computer interaction studies and related fields.

Financial

The *JMIR*'s business model is unique, as it creates revenue streams from personal and institutional memberships. Institutional memberships provide reduced or waived author publication fees for employees of the institution. While HTML versions of all material in the journal are freely available, PDF versions of individual articles, entire issues and topical article collections ('e-collections') are available for a fee (or free to members). An additional revenue stream is the submission and article-processing fees for authors who are not from member institutions, as well as an optional fast-track fee. The journal also accepts advertisements, including Google Adsense, on the website as a source of additional income.

As of January 2007, the journal has almost 600 paying members. As a result, the proportion of funding derived from member contributions is increasing steadily, with over half the revenue coming from memberships and only 25 per cent from article-processing fees in 2007. Between 2004 and 2006 the *JMIR* doubled its total revenue (Gunther Eysenbach, personal communication).

The *JMIR*, like the other OA journals described in this chapter, relies on volunteer effort. The journal also uses paid professionals for some of the more technical aspects of publishing, such as web development, copy-editing and

XML tagging of the articles. These professionals account for the bulk of the journal's expenses.

Review process

Manuscripts are first reviewed by the editor, who decides whether a manuscript meets the criteria specified in the instructions for authors and whether it fits within the scope of the journal. Manuscripts are then sent to an external expert for peer review. Authors are required to suggest at least two peer reviewers. The identity of *JMIR* reviewers is revealed if the manuscript is published (they are acknowledged in each manuscript), unless requested otherwise by the reviewer, but they are anonymous during the review process and in case of rejection. Approximately 30–40 per cent of unsolicited articles are accepted for publication. The *JMIR* uses a customized version of the Open Journal System (OJS), a widely used and very sophisticated open source journal management system available from the Public Knowledge Project (www.webcitation.org/5MvErB1Hy), and also contributes by donating the code developed for the journal as open source to the OJS project. For example, the XML/PDF functionality of the OJS was developed by the *JMIR* group.

The *JMIR* seeks to review and publish manuscripts very quickly. If authors choose to pay for the journal's 'fast-track' review option, a publication decision is guaranteed in ten working days and publication within four weeks. Otherwise, the journal attempts to complete the review and publication process as quickly as possible but does not guarantee a specific timeline. Authors are expected to disclose conflicts of interest and to have received appropriate human subject review approval before conducting research involving human subjects. The journal uses screening software to check for plagiarism of material published on the web, and is a founding member of the WebCite consortium (www.webcitation.org), which supports permanent archiving of web material cited by authors.

Rights management

JMIR papers are published under the Creative Commons Attribution License. The license grants others permission to use the content in whole or in part, and ensures that the original authors and the journal are properly credited/cited when content is used. It grants others permission to redistribute the content. Authors are requested not to publish the same article in another journal.

Editorial board/governance

Gunther Eysenbach is the founder, editor and publisher of the *JMIR*. In addition, the journal has an elected editorial board with responsibilities such as acting as section editors overseeing the review process for specific sets of manuscripts. The journal also seeks guest editors interested in compiling special themed issues.

Indexing/archiving

The *JMIR* is indexed or abstracted in a wide variety of bibliographic databases, reference sources and alert services, including Medline. It also deposits full-text articles in PubMed Central. It is the most widely indexed journal of the five described in this chapter; this in part reflects its multidisciplinary scope. A full listing of these services can be

found on the journal website (www.webcitation.org/
5NwssREcf), which also includes a description of each
service. The *JMIR* is also listed in the ISI's Web of Science
and will receive its first official impact factor (expected to be
around 3.0) in mid-2007.

Structure, content and formatting

The *JMIR*'s article section is organized into yearly volumes
and quarterly issues. Open access versions of articles are
published in HTML. PDF versions are available for a fee
and to individual and institutional members. A variety of
manuscript formats are published, including editorials,
original articles, viewpoints, literature reviews, short papers
and letters.

First Monday

History

In the summer of 1995 Edward J. Valauskas presented a
proposal to the Danish publisher Munksgaard to start a new
internet-only peer-reviewed journal about the internet.
Munksgaard agreed to publish the journal, with Professor
Valauskas as the senior editor. The name *First Monday* was
chosen to reflect the fact that issues would be published on
the first Monday of each month. The first issue was
announced and disseminated at the Fifth International
World Wide Web Conference in Paris, on 6 May 1996.

The original publication model devised by Munksgaard
provided open access to *First Monday* (www.firstmonday
.org/) for its first year if readers registered with Munksgaard
and secured a password. A subscription fee of DK100 was

suggested, but not required. In 1997, on its first anniversary, open access to the entire content of *First Monday* was provided, without passwords or fees.

In 1998 Munksgaard sold *First Monday* to Valauskas and the other senior editors of the journal, Esther Dyson and Rishab Aiyer Ghosh. The journal was moved to the University of Illinois at Chicago and the technical staff of the library agreed to provide a server and support for *First Monday*. This support has continued to this day.

The first successful First Monday conference took place in November 2001 in Maastricht, the Netherlands, at the International Institute of Infonomics. To celebrate *First Monday*'s tenth birthday in 2006, a second First Monday conference was held at the University of Illinois at Chicago on 15–17 May. The theme of the conference was 'Openness: Code, science and content'. Papers from the conference were published in the June and July 2006 issues of *First Monday*.

Scope

First Monday publishes articles on all aspects of the internet, including comments on trends and standards, technical issues, political and social implications and educational uses. Its focus is simply on interesting and novel ideas related to the history, current use and future of the internet.

Financial

First Monday operates largely on the volunteer effort of its editors and editorial board. The journal receives technical support for hosting the journal and other web-based services from the University of Illinois at Chicago Library, through its library systems team. The journal received support from the John D. and Catherine T. MacArthur Foundation and the Open Society Institute for hosting *First Monday*'s tenth anniversary conference.

Review process

The review process is conducted entirely by e-mail. Articles are submitted to the editorial office and from there disseminated to reviewers and the editorial board. The publication decision and, where appropriate, revision process are conducted via e-mail. The journal provides an extensive set of guidelines for authors, covering style and format issues as well as suggestions on how to write for electronic publication.

Rights management

First Monday acquires a limited license to publish from the author. Authors are given the choice of publishing their manuscript under any rights management policy they choose. The instructions to authors encourage use of one of the Creative Commons licenses. The journal issues are copyrighted by the journal, and *First Monday* requests that permission to reprint or use full issues of the journal be referred to the editor. Requests for the use of individual articles are directed to the author.

First Monday has a written statement about privacy that explicitly states the type of information it collects and does not collect about readers and contributors. Essentially, individual information concerning access is not collected. Server logs are kept and analyzed to determine usage patterns for research and improving the site. The journal does maintain a listserv for notifying subscribers about the content of new issues. The e-mail addresses of subscribers will not be disclosed to third parties.

Editorial board/governance

First Monday has a chief editor and eight associate editors, a number of whom handle specific aspects of the editorial process, such as book reviews, legal issues and art. The journal also has a very diverse 17-member editorial board. The journal offices and server are housed within the University of Illinois at Chicago Library.

Indexing/archiving

First Monday is indexed in Communication Abstracts, Computer & Communications Security Abstracts, DoIS, eGranary Digital Library, INSPEC, Information Science & Technology Abstracts, LISA, PAIS and other services.

Structure, content and formatting

First Monday is organized into yearly volumes and monthly issues. Each issue appears on the first Monday of the month. In addition, at various times special issues covering specific topics are published, usually with a guest editor. Articles are published in HTML. The journal publishes peer-reviewed articles and occasional book reviews.

Journal of Electronic Publishing

History

The *Journal of Electronic Publishing* (www.hti.umich.edu/j/jep/) was created by the head of the University of Michigan Press,

Colin Day, in January 1995. He was its first editor, and produced the first two issues. His goal was to explore electronic publishing and other innovations in contemporary publishing practices, and the impact of these practices on users. In 1997 he beguiled Judith Axler Turner, former director of electronic publishing for the *Chronicle of Higher Education*, to take over as editor of the journal, and it went to a regular quarterly publishing schedule. In 2003 the University of Michigan Press agreed to transfer the journal to Columbia University Press, but the transfer was never completed and the journal was not published again until 2006, when it was relaunched by the University of Michigan Library's Scholarly Publishing Office with a new editorial board. Ms Turner continues to edit the journal with the help of contributing editors and staff from the Scholarly Publishing Office and the University of Michigan Library.

Scope

The *JEP* is a forum for research and discussion about contemporary publishing practices, both scholarly and commercial, and the impact of those practices upon users. As the internet has grown, so has the definition of 'publishing', encompassing search engines, blogs and yet-to-be-identified formats as well as traditional scholarly publishing. The journal's audience includes publishers, scholars, librarians, journalists, students, technologists, attorneys, retailers and others with an interest in the methods and means of contemporary publishing.

Financial

The *JEP* is published by the Scholarly Publishing Office with partial support from the University of Michigan Library.

The journal also receives support through sponsorship from ten major commercial publishers and information providers, each of which has a page on the *JEP* site with links to their own websites. Sponsorship is used to support travel to conferences for the editor and SPO staff, who use the opportunity to solicit articles, promote the journal and keep up with the field.

Editors are volunteers, as are members of the editorial board; the publisher, Shana Kimball, works for the Scholarly Publishing Office and her activities are part of her job. The Scholarly Publishing Office makes its publishing system available to the *JEP* free of charge.

The *JEP* encourages readers to become subscribers. Subscribers receive e-mail alerts when issues are published. The journal has about 1,000 subscribers, but most readers get to the *JEP* through internet search engines (the *JEP* comes up first on Google for 'electronic publishing').

Review process

The *JEP* publishes both peer-reviewed and invited papers. Editorial board members provide most of the peer reviews; outside reviewers are solicited when articles are in areas beyond the specific competencies of the editorial board members. All peer review is anonymous, although some reviewers have on occasion offered authors the opportunity to contact them directly. Reviews are anonymized and shared with other reviewers as well as with authors. The editor also reviews and subsequently edits all articles. All related correspondence is conducted via e-mail, and the process is managed by the editor.

Rights management

JEP authors retain their copyright; the *JEP* asks for exclusive rights for 30 days, but that is not a requirement for publication. The *JEP* occasionally republishes articles to give them broader circulation; authors are responsible for getting copyright permission in those cases, and the articles are identified as having been published elsewhere first.

Editorial board/governance

The *JEP* is operated by the Scholarly Publishing Office of the University of Michigan Library. As noted, Judith Axler Turner is the editor. There are several additional editors from the Scholarly Publishing Office and the University of Michigan Library. The journal has a very diverse and distinguished 12-member editorial board who also write for the journal, do peer reviews and provide advice. The content and tone of each issue of the journal are determined by the editor, Ms Turner.

Indexing/archiving

The *JEP* is not currently indexed or archived, although the journal is seeking indexing this year, having finally amassed a large enough body of articles to appeal to indexers.

Structure, content and formatting

The *JEP* is organized into yearly volumes; initially quarterly, it is now published three times a year. Manuscripts are published in HTML. The journal publishes both peer-reviewed and invited articles. The core of each issue is a set of short invited contributions from expert and experienced practitioners on a particular theme. The journal also seeks out and encourages longer pieces from scholars and others. Most issues include an editorial summarizing the theme and introducing the articles contained in the issue.

Summary

Although this is a very small, non-random sample, a number of interesting themes can be seen in these journals. First, they appear to share many of the characteristics Jill Coffin has identified in open source software projects and has hypothesized to provide a more general framework for diverse collaborative communities (Coffin, 2006). Scholarly journals, and in particular OA journals, are in essence collaborative projects where, like open source software projects, a large number of people share in the development and dissemination of intellectual property and take ownership of the project at some level. Like typical open source projects, each of these journals, with possibly the exception of the *JEP*, has a leader (editor) who was the central figure in starting the journal and continues to be the central force in maintaining it. OA journals are also based on geographically distributed, asynchronous, networked collaboration and incorporate peer review as a quality control mechanism, all characteristics Coffin has identified in open source projects. In my experience, like open source projects, there is a community-wide sense of ownership among readers, reviewers and those more actively involved in maintaining an OA journal. As with open source projects, each of these journals has a core group of very committed people who, with the editor, largely determine the direction and ethos of the project, and a much larger group of supporters who donate time and effort but are far less involved.

Publishing a journal requires resources. Electronic publication and use of electronic communication to conduct peer reviews have drastically reduced the resources required, but publishing a scholarly journal still requires substantial resources. Since OA journals make their content freely available they have no natural income stream. OA journals have at their disposal three general options for obtaining the resources necessary to publish. First, they can seek income though author fees, advertising or the sale of added-value products. Second, they can seek subsidies in the form of money or services from various private organizations, foundations and/or governmental agencies. Third, they can operate on volunteer labor. Each of the journals has addressed the issue of obtaining the necessary resources to operate somewhat differently.

The *JMIR* funds many of the technical aspects of operating the journal through publication fees, the sale of added-value products, memberships and advertising. These are strategies commonly used in larger commercial or society-based organizations that publish OA journals, such as BioMed Central and the PLoS.

The *JEP* derives most of its support in the form of subsidies. It was initiated and continues to be maintained by an academic library, and in addition receives subsidies from a number of commercial publishing companies. This is also a common model, and a growing number of academic libraries have begun to collaborate with faculty at their institutions in publishing OA journals. This is a natural evolution of academic libraries, which have a strong interest in promoting OA publishing as well as having the resources and expertise to help support the development and operation of OA journals. *MEO*, *First Monday* and *IR* are largely operated on volunteer effort by their editors and a small group of colleagues with a very limited amount of technical support or subsidies. Again, this is a common model.

Garnering resources, whether in cash or other forms of support, is one of the most challenging aspects of operating an OA journal. There is no correct way to secure the necessary resources it takes to operate a journal. Each of the three general sources of support has its strengths and weaknesses. This topic will be discussed in detail in Chapter 6.

The majority of the material in each of these journals is peer reviewed. Though a slightly lower percentage of OA journals are peer reviewed as compared with fee-for-access journals, the majority of OA journals are peer reviewed (Kaufman-Will Group, 2005). Three of the journals conduct the review process via e-mail. *MEO* has used a web-based peer-review system developed in-house, and *IR* is in the process of implementing the OJS. As will be discussed in more detail in Chapter 4, web-based peer-review systems can significantly streamline the process as well as providing automated tracking of manuscripts during the entire pre-publication process. Even just conducting the peer-review process via e-mail rather than paper saves considerable resources and effort.

All the journals with the exception of *MEO* are published in some version of HTML. *MEO* is published in PDF and the *JMIR* is available in PDF for a fee to help defray the cost of operating the journal. The *JMIR*'s practice of charging for access to the PDF versions as an added-value feature is not uncommon. Other well-known journals such as *Postgraduate Medicine* use this strategy to allow open access for their content while generating income for operating the journal. While an excellent choice for distributing high-quality printable versions of articles, PDF format does have some disadvantages, particularly for long-term archiving and indexing. Only the *JMIR* creates XML versions of its material for indexing and archiving. This is a time-consuming technical process requiring significant resources.

The advantages and disadvantages of various publication formats will be discussed in more detail in Chapters 4 and 9.

The five journals discussed in this chapter are all examples of well-established and widely read OA journals that publish high-quality peer-reviewed articles on a par with traditional fee-for-access journals. With the exception of the *JEP* and *First Monday*, the individuals who started these journals are faculty members without experience or specific expertise in publishing. They demonstrate that while not easy, it can be done. Each of them has approached the challenges of garnering the necessary resources and operating a peer-reviewed scholarly journal in very different ways. There are a variety of options for designing and operating an OA journal. Each has its advantages and disadvantages, and we are all continuing to learn how to do it better. The goal of the rest of this book is to help you through the decision process of designing and operating your own journal.

Note

1. This chapter borrows liberally from the text on the websites of these journals. This is done with permission of the editors of each journal.

Part II
Crafting a new open access journal

3

Journal planning issues

The first two chapters of this book provided background material for those interested in starting a new electronic OA journal. In this chapter we begin discussing the actual process of creating an OA journal and some of the issues you should consider.

At this point it is a good idea to think through carefully why you want to start a new journal. What are your goals, rationale and motivation for embarking on this process? While I in no way mean to discourage you from moving forward in creating a new journal, it is hard to overemphasize the fact that this endeavor should be considered a major, long-term commitment and the decision to start a journal should not be made lightly. If you create a journal and start accepting and publishing manuscripts, you have a very real commitment to both the authors and your profession to maintain the manuscripts you publish indefinitely and work to ensure the long-term success of the new journal. Authors put a tremendous amount of work into their articles, which play a very important role in the success of their careers in academia. By submitting their manuscripts for publication in your journal, they are entrusting you with something that is of great value to them. As a publisher, if you agree to publish their manuscripts you have an obligation to maintain both the availability of the articles published through your journal and to do your best to ensure that the journal thrives.

As discussed in Chapter 1, journals form the basis of our archive of knowledge and it is critical that the archive remains intact and accessible. So not only do you have an obligation to the authors who entrust their manuscripts to you, but also to your profession in helping to maintain the archive of knowledge in the field. Chapter 7 discusses the various options for archiving the manuscripts that will be published in your journal. Beyond permanent archiving, which will ensure the long-term survival of the manuscripts you publish, you also have an obligation to the authors who publish in your journal to maintain the journal itself. Journals 'brand' the articles they publish with the journal's reputation. I suspect the whole notion of 'core journals' and impact factors will fade over time as people realize electronic publication provides the ability to create more relevant measures of impact at the article rather than the journal level. But at the present time the credit authors receive for publishing in your journal will be significantly tied to the reputation of the journal. For that reason, you have an obligation when you start a journal to do your best to see it continues to flourish and develops a good reputation.

As we saw with the five journals discussed in the last chapter, OA journals are often started and largely maintained by a single central figure. Having played this role with *MEO*, I would urge you not to try to go it alone when starting an OA journal. As your journal becomes successful, as it most likely will over time, the workload is too much for a single person. It is also relentless and uncontrollable, largely determined by the decision of authors to submit their manuscripts for publication in your journal. It is far easier to have other people who can help when the workload spikes or you are sick or busy with other things.

Determining the name and scope of the journal

One of the first things you should think about in developing a journal is coming up with a name and defining the scope. Obviously this should flow from your goals in starting the journal. The name in particular should be chosen with a great deal of care and forethought, as well as some research. It will play a significant role in defining the journal to both potential readers and authors. It 'brands' the journal, and it will be very difficult and disruptive to change the name once the journal becomes established. It can also create a whole lot of trouble if you are not careful in ensuring you are not trespassing on someone else's intellectual property. You obviously want the name to be descriptive and to convey clearly and unambiguously the scope and focus of the journal. It is also helpful to have a name that is easy to remember or has an acronym that grabs one's attention.

It is very important to do some research to ensure the name is not in use or too similar to the name of another journal or other entity. The last thing you want to do is cause confusion or get into a dispute over the rights to the name of the journal. I ran into this problem with *MEO*. There is another very well-known journal in medical education called *Medical Education*, published by Blackwell. While I was very aware of the journal when I started *MEO*, it did not dawn on me that it would cause any confusion. A few years after I started *MEO* I began to receive submissions where the authors thought they were submitting their articles to *Medical Education* or the 'online version' of *Medical Education*. This was happening several times a year, and in some cases the manuscripts got through the full peer-review process before the authors realized their mistake and asked to withdraw the manuscripts. Early on I added text to both the homepage and instructions to authors making it clear *Medical Education Online* was not affiliated with *Medical Education*. Unfortunately the confusion continued. A couple of years ago, out of frustration, I stated this in bold red large-point text at the beginning of the instructions for authors, and it seems to have finally got the message across – we have not received any more submissions intended for *Medical Education*.

I have been in contact with the editors of *Medical Education* at various times and they are aware of the problem. Fortunately they have always been very gracious, and they as well as Blackwell have never asserted their rights to the name and demanded I change the name of *MEO*, which I would have little recourse but to do. This is clearly a situation you want to avoid. Not only does such confusion cause problems for everyone involved, but if the other journal or entity chooses to demand you change the name of your journal you will probably have to comply.

Carefully choosing how you define the scope of the new journal is also important. The scope will convey to potential authors and readers the content of the journal. Obviously it needs to reflect the goals for the journal. The statement of the journal's scope should be as clear and unambiguous as possible. This will avoid confusion and wasted time for authors as well as yourself by helping to ensure that the manuscripts submitted to the journal are appropriate. It is also helpful to keep the statement of the scope short and concise so it can be easily read and interpreted. You may wish to develop a brief, concise statement of the scope that you can place in prominent places such as the homepage of your journal's website, and to develop a more in-depth statement that helps clarify the scope in the instructions to authors.

It is necessary to consider the breadth of the scope. You want it broad enough to ensure there will be a reasonable number of submissions and the journal will be of interest to a significant number of people, while not so broad that the journal does not have a clear focus. It is helpful to consider the other journals in the field. As an expert, you are probably familiar with the key journals in your area. While in most fields there is room for some overlap, starting a new journal in an area that is already saturated with existing journals will be very challenging. As it is, authors are hesitant to submit their manuscripts to a new journal and it is always an uphill battle to become established. If authors already have plenty of options, it will be all the more challenging to garner enough submissions to become established. Your job will be considerably easier if you can find a niche your journal can fill that is needed in your field. Fortunately, being the only OA journal in your field may provide a unique niche as more and more scholars become familiar with the arguments for OA. This advantage, however, may be short-lived, as there is increasing pressure on journals to become OA.

Determining an organizational and governance structure

Your journal will need some type of organizational and governance structure. The nature of that structure will depend on your situation and plans for the journal. If you are planning on starting the new journal yourself or with a few colleagues, and operating the journal largely on volunteer effort, the organizational and governance structure can be very simple and informal. If you are planning on developing a journal on a larger scale, using a paid staff or contracting out services such as copy-editing, indexing and/or web hosting, you will need a more clearly defined entity and governance structure to handle the financial and management issues necessary to operate a journal with a significant budget. If your journal is going to be operated by an existing entity, such as a professional society or university department, you can incorporate the journal's organizational structure into the organizational structure of the entity that is operating the journal. This will simplify your task, particularly in terms of financial issues of accounting and taxes.

Although a new journal will start out as a small operation that can easily be managed with a very informal structure, it is a good idea to look farther down the road to when the journal is likely to be a bigger enterprise. It is certainly possible to operate a journal without a budget totally on volunteer effort, but in most cases your journal will have some cashflow and will need an accounting structure to support it. Depending on the country in which you are located, with a cashflow there may well be tax issues that need to be addressed. It is a good idea to develop a set of by-laws or some other defined structure outlining procedures for operating the journal, as well as specific journal policies. This issue is discussed in considerable depth in Chapter 5.

Forming an editorial board

Traditionally, scholarly journals have an editorial board that advises the editors and helps develop the journal's policies and direction. Editorial boards also often play a significant role in the peer-review process. There is no hard-and-fast rule that says you must have an editorial board, nor any specific requirements for its structure, make-up and role. I strongly suggest you consider having some type of editorial board. As mentioned above, the board can provide you with support, help and advice. Additionally, the members' reputations and contacts can go a long way in helping you get the journal up and running. Starting a journal creates a 'chicken-and-egg' problem of developing a reputation that will ensure a steady stream of submissions. Most authors are reluctant to submit manuscripts, particularly their best manuscripts, to a new journal without a reputation. At the same time, a new journal cannot develop a good reputation unless it receives and publishes high-quality manuscripts. The efforts of a strong editorial board whose members are well respected in their disciplines can go a long way to encouraging wary authors to submit their manuscripts to your new journal. They can act as a network promoting the journal and encouraging colleagues to submit their manuscripts to your new journal. There is also a general expectation that journals will have an editorial board, and this can influence your ability to get the journal indexed. For example, PubMed Central specifies as one of its criteria for accepting new journals that three members of the journal's editorial board have significant grant funding.

In forming your editorial board, you obviously want people who are well known and respected in the field. You also want people who are thoughtful and can provide good advice and help you in designing policies and in making the important decisions on how you structure and operate the journal. Many journals also use their editorial boards in reviewing and selecting manuscripts. If you choose to use the editorial board in this fashion, you obviously want people who have the time and willingness to take on this role. In addition, you will need people who will complete these tasks in a timely fashion.

If you are involved in an organization that is developing a new journal, the source of the editorial board could be largely predetermined. If not, you will have to seek members for the board. This can be easier than you might think. Being asked to be on an editorial board, even for a new journal, is an honor. Given how critical the board can be to the success of the journal, do not hesitate to ask well-known people in your field. Even if they do not accept, you have lost nothing – and you are likely to be pleasantly surprised. You may consider not asking the board to be involved in the review of manuscripts, or making it optional, so that you do not exclude well-known people who are generally busy and may not want or have the time to be involved in manuscript review.

Defining a peer-review policy

The vast majority of scholarly journals are peer reviewed, and there are many compelling reasons for you to include some type of peer-review process for evaluating manuscripts. When considering a peer-review policy it is helpful to consider the five roles journals play in scholarly communities, discussed in Chapter 1, and how you envision your journal fitting in among these. While most journals tend to fulfill all the roles to some extent, you may wish to focus on a subset of roles in designing a new journal.

Peer review plays a key role in ensuring the journal articles that make up our archive of knowledge are accurate and fit with established practices for scholarship and research in a particular field. It should be noted that there is some controversy over the effectiveness of peer review in fulfilling this role (Pocock et al., 1987; Gøtzsche, 1989; Baxt et al., 1998). But despite its flaws, peer review is still probably the best mechanism we have for ensuring the accuracy and appropriateness of scholarly information (Jefferson, 2006).

Peer review also plays an important part in distributing rewards and credit for scholarly work. This of itself is a compelling reason to include peer review as a feature in a new scholarly journal. The authors who publish in your journal will get little credit for their manuscripts if they are published in a not-peer-reviewed journal, and for this reason you are likely to have trouble attracting high-quality manuscripts for your journal if it is not peer reviewed.

Another important reason for implementing peer review is that the constructive feedback and advice provided by reviewers generally results in a much better manuscript being published than was first submitted. I am continually amazed at the thought and effort many (not all) reviewers put into the review process. In my experience, authors generally appreciate the feedback even when their manuscripts are not accepted for publication. The net result of this feedback is almost inevitably a significantly better manuscript. Everyone has a point of view and biases. The best way to address this is to have multiple experts review and provide feedback on a manuscript.

While the peer-review process in the past took significant resources, the web has taken much of the clerical and administrative work out of the process. Simply conducting the peer review via e-mail rather that postal mail will both significantly reduce the effort and dramatically reduce the cost of conducting peer review. Using web-based database-driven peer-review software can go significantly further in improving the efficiency, eliminating virtually all the clerical and administrative effort of the review process and leaving only the actual review effort and the effort of the editor to oversee and manage the process. This software can also track manuscripts through the peer-review process, helping ensure they are not lost or sidetracked and that authors receive feedback in a timely fashion. Options for peer-review management software will be discussed in more detail in the next chapter, but it is something you should definitely consider in designing a new journal.

You will also have to decide how you will recruit and select peer reviewers. Your editorial board can serve as one source of peer reviewers; however, unless your journal has a very large editorial board, you will probably need additional experts to keep the workload of the review process reasonable. Most journals solicit well-known experts in their scholarly field to act as peer reviewers. There should be enough reviewers available to ensure no one gets overworked. Reviewers vary in how much they are willing to review – probably three or four articles a year is the maximum you should expect any one reviewer to take on.

Soliciting reviewers can potentially be challenging if you wish to be selective, as most editors prefer to be. Using your informal networks is one source of reviewers. Most fields have listservs and/or bulletin boards that are used by people within the field. That is another potential means of soliciting people to volunteer to review. If your journal is associated with a society, the membership list is another good source of reviewers. Authors of articles published in your journal are also a potential source of reviewers. This is a strategy that has been used quite effectively by the *JMIR*, one of the journals discussed in Chapter 2. Advertising on the journal website for reviewers is a strategy we have used with some success for *MEO*.

You will also need to gather information about potential reviewers' areas of expertise and interest to determine which manuscripts to assign to them. This can be as simple as having them provide a copy of their curriculum vitae when indicating their interest in reviewing. For efficiency it is helpful to have them enter this information via a web-based form so it can be input directly into a database and is easily accessible to the editor when assigning reviewers to a manuscript. The issue of automating and streamlining the review process will be discussed in more detail in the next chapter.

Although most journals attempt to seek well-known people in the field for reviewing manuscripts, we have taken a somewhat different approach for *MEO*. We solicit reviewers on the journal website and occasionally, as needed, via a popular listserv in the field, asking them to complete a web form with their interests and expertise if they would like to be considered as a reviewer for the journal. While we screen the completed forms, we add any person who offers to review to our database as long as they supply sufficient information and appear to be legitimately interested in reviewing for the journal. When assigning reviewers, we try to assign several experienced reviewers who we know do a good job and add in some new reviewers as well. This gives us a chance to see how the new people perform, while ensuring we have feedback from trusted reviewers for each manuscript.

MEO uses highly automated web-based peer-review software, so it is possible to assign a large number (usually six or more) of reviewers without substantially increasing the workload for the review editor. With our relatively open review policy, the journal has in excess of 300 registered reviewers, so it is also possible to assign a large number of reviewers without overburdening individual reviewers.

Another factor allowing this approach to work is that our review software makes it easy for editors to view the history of each reviewer when assigning reviews, including the number of times they have been asked to review, whether they accepted requests to review and if/when they returned the review. The editors can also easily add comments on the quality of the review to a reviewer's data record, which is available to all our review editors when assigning reviewers.

The system works quite well. Of course a number of the people who sign up to review never accept reviewing requests, fail to return reviews they accept and/or do a poor job of reviewing. Since we always try to include experienced and trusted reviewers, there is almost always an adequate amount of good-quality feedback available to the review editors. The system quickly identifies individuals in our review database who are poor reviewers, and these people are periodically deleted from the database by the managing editors. We also have a lot of pleasant surprises, where the people signing up to review turn out to be superb reviewers providing lots of insightful feedback.

There is also a growing interest in open review, and several major journals have been experimenting with various forms of this (Solomon, 2007). At one end of the spectrum, open review refers to simply making public the identities of the reviewers and/or letting the reviewers know the identity of the authors of the manuscript they are reviewing. More recently, with the availability of web-based review systems, journals are experimenting with publishing as 'pre-print' manuscripts that have not been peer reviewed, allowing public comment on these manuscripts and then using the public comment – possibly along with assigned reviewers – in determining whether a manuscript should be published. For a three-month period during the summer of 2006, *Nature* experimented with a form of open peer review. The editors did not feel it was successful and dropped the project: the public response rate was too low and the comments that were provided tended to be superficial (Brown, 2007). Several smaller journals have used variations of this model with more success. In addition the Public Library of Science, which publishes a number of very well-respected OA journals, has started *PLoS One*, which does not perform traditional peer review. Manuscripts are screened to ensure they are appropriate scientific articles and are published almost immediately. The journal uses a range of tools to promote interactive discussion among readers concerning the articles, even allowing registered scientists to annotate directly in the web versions of the manuscripts. While these experiments in new forms of peer review and commentary are intriguing, it would probably be a good idea to get your journal off the ground using a more traditional peer-review model and then consider experimenting with an open review process.

No matter what type of peer-review system you choose for your journal, an editor who is experienced and well versed in the field is an essential ingredient for an effective peer-review process. While individual reviewers generally provide useful, often insightful information, there are differences of opinion and perspective among reviewers, occasionally contradictory suggestions and sometimes the feedback provided is just plain wrong. It is not that the editor is necessarily any less fallible than the reviewers, but someone has to take charge, sort through the feedback and provide a clear statement of what must be addressed by the author for the manuscript to be published. Otherwise, it just drives authors crazy.

As your journal grows and with it the work required to manage the editorial process, you may consider moving to a multilevel editorial system with multiple review editors to handle the required effort. This can be done in a variety of ways. You can have section editors who manage the review of specific sections of the journal, such as book reviews, review articles and research articles. It is also possible to have a number of review editors without specific assignments to sections and have manuscripts assigned to them by a managing editor based on interest and availability. *MEO* uses the latter model, with two managing editors and six review editors. One of the managing editors does an initial review of a submitted manuscript and determines if it is within the scope of the journal and potentially publishable. If not, they send a short e-mail to the author indicating why they felt the manuscript was not publishable in *MEO*. If the manuscript makes it through that initial screen, it is assigned to a review editor, who prepares the manuscript for review, selects the reviewers, monitors the review process, makes a final publication decision based on the feedback from the reviewers and their own assessment of the manuscript, and writes a summary statement to the author. If accepted with revisions, they also manage the revision process.

The model works well for *MEO* and is flexible. It is a relatively simple process to add additional review editors as the number of submissions increases, limiting the workload of any individual editor. The model also has the flexibility to adjust to the schedules of the individual editors. If someone is swamped with work or on vacation, it is possible to assign manuscripts to other reviewers. While it will probably not be necessary to implement a multilevel review system initially, it provides a good option as the workload increases.

You will also need to develop a review form. While some journals just ask reviewers to comment on various aspects of the manuscript, most also include a system for providing numerical ratings. If your form provides numerical rating criteria, be sure to allow and encourage reviewers to provide written feedback as well, as this is likely to be the most helpful for both you and the authors. You may also wish to have the reviewers suggest whether they feel the manuscript should be published, published with revisions or rejected. It is also helpful to include a separate section for comments that are only to be seen by the editor and not passed on to the author.

Journal structure and content

The majority of content in most scholarly journals is peer-reviewed articles submitted by authors; however, most journals include several different types of content and often a variety of formats and/or sections for the peer-reviewed articles that are published. Part of the process of designing a new journal is deciding what type of content the journal will contain and the format of that content. This decision should ultimately be guided by your objectives for the journal. You are probably familiar with a number of scholarly journals and have a pretty good idea of the types of content they contain. It may also be helpful to review other journals in the field or related fields to get some ideas.

Fortunately you can start with a more limited set of content and add features to the journal later after it has become established. Table 3.1 lists some of the more common forms of content in scholarly journals.

Electronic media provide a great deal of flexibility not found in paper publication, and you may wish to consider using the potential of the web to support different types of formats for communication not generally found in traditional journals. At a most basic level, electronic publication does away with limits on the amount of material that can be published. With paper publication the cost of each additional page of material is quite expensive. With electronic publication, massive amounts of material can be published at virtually no cost. This provides the flexibility of

Table 3.1	Common types of scholarly journal content

Article formats

- *Research articles* – High-quality research consistent with the expectations in the field for research design and presentation. Generally peer reviewed.
- *Review articles* – Summaries of the literature, usually with clearly defined criteria for study inclusion and often employing meta-analytic statistical techniques in medicine and the social sciences. Generally peer reviewed.
- *Invited articles* – Generally a well-respected scholar in the field is invited to submit an article in their area of expertise. Generally not peer reviewed.
- *Brief reports* – Short articles usually with specific page/word limits on very focused topics. Often peer reviewed but may not have the same expectations as a research or feature article.
- *Feature articles* – Presentation and discussion of issues of interest in the field. Generally peer reviewed.
- *Editorials* – Commentary from the editor on topics of general interest in the field. Generally not peer reviewed.

Letters to the editor

- Includes opinion papers submitted by authors, generally not peer reviewed but screened by the editor. Some journals will accept certain manuscripts submitted for publication as research or feature articles that were too weak to meet the peer-review requirements but have some value.

Book/software reviews

- Publishers and authors often submit books for review. Editors solicit reviewers who read the book and provide a summary and an evaluation/commentary. Book reviews are generally not peer reviewed but screened by the editor.

Conference proceedings

- Journals affiliated with scholarly societies often publish conference proceedings. These may be the abstracts from presentations given at a meeting, or in some cases a special issue is published with full papers. The papers are often peer reviewed but usually as presentations to be given at the meeting, and may use a different set of reviewers and different set of procedures than used for other articles.

| **Table 3.1** | Common types of scholarly journal content (*Cont'd*) |

Tutorials
■ Though not as common as some of the other sections, some journals include articles that are essentially lessons or tutorials designed to teach a specific set of information or skills, often designed for relatively inexperienced members of the scholarly field.
Announcements or updates
■ Some journals have a section for announcements or updates on various activities or functions in the field. This is probably most common for societal journals.

publishing extensive appendices of reference materials related to articles and even whole datasets and multimedia material. Some journals, such as *Education Policy Analyst Archives* (www.webcitation.org/5Qukfo84y), require authors to publish their datasets. While there are some issues in creating such a mandatory requirement, it has huge benefits in maximizing the value of research, particularly publicly funded research.

Electronic publication also offers the potential of more interactive modes of communication that can enhance the value of your journal. For example, bulletin boards and other software that allows asynchronous interactive discussion where readers can comment on articles and other readers or the author can reply, creating running conversation, could significantly extend the value of the material published in your journal. *MEO* has just implemented such a system as this chapter is being written. While a few readers have begun commenting, it is not clear as yet how successful the system will be over time.

While the web has become an integral part of life for many of us, it is easy to forget it has only been around for about 15 years. We still have a lot to learn in making the best use of electronic media for scholarly communication. I hope you will use your new journal as a means of experimenting with new, innovative ways of communicating.

Format, layout and style

Format

You will need to determine in what digital format(s) the content of the journal will be published. The two most common formats are hypertext markup language (HTML) and portable document format (PDF). Both are reasonable choices, and each has its advantages and disadvantages.

HTML is universal as the predominant format for webpages, relatively compact and quite versatile. Since any computer that can access the web can access an HTML document, publishing in HTML will be universally accessible. Its major disadvantage is the quality and consistency of the resulting document's appearance. It is not possible to achieve the same level of precision in formatting as PDFs created in desktop publishing software or even a word processor. HTML also does not truly support pagination. Although there has been a marked improvement over the last few years, there are distinct differences in how different browsers display HTML.

One of PDF's biggest advantages is that it supports a quality consistent with typeset documents. PDF documents can be generated from the print image produced by any software program. This provides a great deal of flexibility and efficiency. Since the manuscripts you will receive and edit will probably be word processing documents, they can be either formatted for publication in a word possessor and converted to PDF format or transferred to desktop publishing software, formatted and then converted to PDF format. In either case, the result is a substantially higher-quality document than can be achieved in HTML. The majority of readers clearly prefer PDF to HTML format – so much so that journals such as the *JMIR*, described in the previous chapter, provide HTML versions of their manuscripts free of charge yet are still able to charge for the PDF versions as a means of funding the journal.

Many journals produce an additional format specifically for archival purposes, generally in XML. XML is a markup language for documents containing structured information (Walsh, 2007). It is particularly well suited for archival purposes and required for certain archives, such as PubMed Central, a widely used archive for biomedical journals. Creating XML versions of articles is technically more challenging and time-consuming than using HTML or PDF formats.

Layout

You will also need to determine the page layout for articles and other material in the journal. One strategy that can be very helpful in choosing a layout format is to look at the layout of a number of other journals, especially journals in your field or similar fields. This can give you some ideas on how the pages could look. You can then choose from what you feel are the best features of several journals in designing the page layout. Be sure to include the full reference for the articles somewhere in the article so they can be easily located after the article is printed. When creating the layout for PDF versions of articles that are paginated, it is helpful to include the reference on each page in the header or footer of the document. Also, be sure to include page numbers.

Style guide

Finally, it will be necessary to choose a style guide for references, tables and other aspects of the text and language used in the journal. There are general style guides such as the Chicago Manual of Style (2007). In addition, many fields have standard style guides for research and scholarship published in their field, such as the American Psychological Association (APA) style guide that is widely used in the social sciences and the International Committee of Medical Journal Editors *Uniform Requirements for Manuscripts Submitted to Biomedical Journals* (ICMJE, 2007) commonly used in the biomedical field. Much thought and effort have gone into creating these guides, they are readily available and most authors will be familiar with them, so they can serve as a good foundation on which to base your requirements.

Developing instructions for authors

You will need to develop instructions for authors submitting material to the journal. These will provide guidance on the nature and format of the material you will consider for publication, the submission process and relevant journal policies. Instructions for authors are a critical component of the documentation for the journal. Putting some effort into developing a clear and comprehensive set of instructions for authors will help avoid considerable confusion and frustration on the part of authors and the journal's editors.

Chapter 5 contains a detailed discussion of the material that should be contained in the instructions for authors in your new journal.

There are a number of other key issues in planning and implementing a new journal that are complex enough to require their own chapters. These will be covered in the next four chapters.

4

Hosting and data systems

The technical issues of web hosting are one of the challenges you will need to address in setting up your journal. If you have little or no experience in this area, you would be wise to seek out someone with technical expertise to help you through the process. The initial decisions you make in developing your journal can have long-term ramifications and could potentially haunt you for years to come, so it is best to think through the hosting issues carefully before starting a journal.

Paper journals by their nature are incredibly robust. The fact that hundreds if not thousands of copies of each issue of a paper journal are distributed to widely dispersed locations virtually guarantees that the information they contain will never be destroyed. Such robustness is not a natural feature of electronic journals. It is possible to protect the information contained in these journals; but, unlike paper journals, durability is not an inherent feature of the medium. One must explicitly build specific steps to protect material into the process of maintaining an electronic journal. By creating a new electronic journal, you are creating a small piece of our archive of knowledge. You have an obligation both to the authors who entrust their work to your journal and to your scholarly field to ensure that what is published through the journal will always be available to those who wish to access it.

The first part of this chapter will present issues to consider in hosting your journal. These will include the choice of a domain name, options for obtaining web hosting and the selection of software, including a journal management system. The second part of the chapter presents strategies for ensuring the availability and integrity of both the structure of the journal and material contained within it.

Hosting issues

Domain names

As for all websites, uniform resource locators (URLs) are generally used to reference the location of articles in electronic journals. The importance of maintaining the integrity of these URLs cannot be overemphasized. The pervasiveness of broken links (URLs), which once led to an important document and now lead nowhere, is a huge problem. It has become the Achilles' heel of electronic publication. Please do not become part of the problem! You have an obligation not only to ensure the material you publish remains available but also, if at all possible, at the same location at which it was originally published.

The first part of addressing this issue is ensuring the domain name for your journal never changes. The domain name in a URL references the host server (computer) on which a file such as an electronic journal article is located. Files are actually routed between computers on the internet via what is known as an internet protocol (IP) address. Under the current organization of the internet, this is a 32-bit or 4-byte binary number, usually expressed in what is termed 'dot-decimal' notation, which might look something like '35.8.143.13'. Since it is much easier for humans to use a name as opposed to a large number, domain names are generally used in place of IP addresses in a URL. This is accomplished through a system of name servers that act as cross-reference tables, allowing computers to obtain the IP address associated with a particular domain name.

Domain names have other important benefits. They provide a means of 'branding' websites as well as conveniently accessing them. This is very useful in commerce, but will also allow you to have a domain name for your new journal that is easily remembered and reflects the content of the journal. The other very valuable aspect of a domain name is that it allows you to move a website from server to server without altering the URL *even though the IP address has changed*. There is a relatively straightforward process where you can submit a request to change the IP address associated with a domain name that is stored in the name servers on the internet. This allows you to move your journal from server to server in a way that is completely transparent to the people who access the journal.

The second part of ensuring the viability of the URLs for the articles and other material contained in your journal is to maintain a consistent organizational structure for the journal's website. Since part of the URL is the path to the resource (file) in the internal file structure of your website on the server, any change in the organizational structure of the site or name of the file containing a journal article or other material will result in a change in the URL.

Most web developers organize the material in a website into a series of hierarchical folders. Some journal management software will take care of this issue for you but, if not, think through carefully how you want to organize your journal website *before creating it*. Once you begin adding articles and other material, you will not be able to reorganize the website without changing the URLs of the material in the site. It is possible to program a web server to redirect a request from the original URL to the new location if the location of a file has changed; however, this is cumbersome and not always effective. *The best option is to think through carefully how you want to organize your site before it is developed, and stick with it.* It is hard to overemphasize this point.

When starting a new journal you can either use an existing domain name that is already in use for the server on which the journal will be maintained or purchase a new domain name specifically for the journal. In most instances, it is best to purchase a new domain name. First, it will allow you to choose a name that describes the scope and content of the journal. Ideally the domain name can augment the 'branding' of the journal. Secondly, it will allow you to move the journal to a different server while maintaining the same domain name. Over time, it is quite likely you will want or even need to do this. Over its 11-year history, *MEO* has been maintained on seven different servers. Purchasing a domain name is easy and inexpensive. There are hundreds of domain registrars that will allow you to register a domain name, and it is possible to purchase a domain name for less than US$10.00 per year. Choosing a registrar is discussed in more detail below.

Selecting a server

If you are a faculty member in a college or university, it is quite likely your institution will allow you to use space on one of their servers for hosting your journal. While each IP address refers to a specific computer or other device on the internet or other network, most server software is designed to support multiple domain names, sometimes with their own unique IP address and sometimes not. It is quite possible for a single physical computer to act as a server for dozens or even hundreds of websites, each with a different domain name. While technically it should be feasible for your institution to host a separate domain name for your journal, policies vary from institution to institution on whether they will allow you to purchase and host your own domain name on their servers or require that you use the institution's domain name. In most situations I strongly suggest you purchase a separate domain name for the journal for the reasons cited above. If your institution will not host your own domain name, you should seriously consider using another hosting option. The one exception to this rule is if the journal by design is clearly affiliated with the institution – for example, if the journal is going to be sponsored by a department or a college. In this case it does make sense to use the institution's URL for the journal since the intent is to 'brand' the journal as affiliated with the institution. Additionally, if the journal is closely tied to the institution, it is unlikely that there will ever be a reason to move the journal to a server outside the institution, requiring that the domain name change.

If hosting the journal via one of your institution's servers does not appear to be a good option, the cost of using a commercial web hosting service for your journal site is very reasonable and there are hundreds from which you can choose. There is fierce completion among web hosting companies, and the cost of hosting has dropped substantially over the last few years while the resources these companies provide for their hosting accounts have increased dramatically. In most cases, even a hosting company's least expensive hosting option can provide more than adequate resources for even a well-established and highly accessed journal. Most of these companies are also domain registrars, so it is possible to obtain your domain name and your web hosting account through the same company. This generally simplifies the process, though it is not necessary, and if you decide in the future to switch to another company you can take the journal's domain with you.

Finding a good hosting company and domain registrar is important. There are several issues to consider, including support, performance, adequate resources, ease of use, software and of course price. There are many websites that rate and compare web hosting providers and can help you make a good decision as to where to host your journal. Most of these sites provide some means for people to comment on their experiences with a particular company. Just type something like 'web hosting reviews' into a search engine such as Google and you will get a list of such sites. In my experience these comments are one of the best sources of information on web-based services, including hosting companies. I suggest going with a large hosting company with a track record, based on reviews and users' comments. It is less likely to go out of business or have the quality of its services drop in this fiercely competitive market. The large, well-established companies that have been in business for a while should have comments from hundreds of users on these review sites. There are always a few unhappy people no matter how good a company is, but if there are hundreds of reviews and the vast majority are positive and fairly consistent, you are likely to have a good experience with that vendor.

Support is one of the most important considerations in choosing a hosting company. Even if you are an experienced web developer, there are likely to be times when you will need to contact the support personnel. If you are a novice, you may quickly get to be on first-name terms with the support staff. Having accessible and competent phone and e-mail support is essential. Most hosting companies provide support 24 hours a day, seven days a week, and the good ones respond quickly to your requests. Since it is quite possible the company you choose will be in another time zone, possibly on the other side of the world, 24-hour support can be important. The other issue, of course, is competence of the support team. The best way to assess the quality and responsiveness of a provider's support is by the comments of other users.

A second issue is performance. You want a hosting service that has a good connection to the main internet backbone, rare outages and does not overload its servers to the point where they are not responsive to user requests for webpages. Fortunately, most hosting companies these days provide good performance or they just do not stay in business. It can potentially be an issue, however, and I have had to move *MEO* to a different web hosting company twice largely because of performance problems.

Occasionally a previously well-run hosting company goes downhill fast. You are likely to be accessing your journal often enough to have an idea if the journal's site is having access problems. You will probably eventually hear from your readers via e-mail if access is consistently a problem. Unfortunately, most people accessing your journal will not complain, and server performance issues, particularly frequent outages, can severely damage the reputation of your journal and its growth. If you suspect there are hosting problems, check your journal site regularly and be prepared to move your journal to another hosting service. The process is usually not too difficult and is discussed in more detail below.

A third issue is the ease with which you can manage a web hosting account. Hosting companies usually provide what is called a 'control panel' for managing your hosting account and site. This is a webpage or series of webpages that allows you to view and manipulate various settings and monitor the use of resources on the website. Tasks such as setting passwords, creating e-mail accounts and monitoring resources are examples of the management activities that are done through a hosting company's control panel. In addition, hosting companies often offer software utilities that can be accessed through their control panels, such as software for creating and restoring archives, creating protected directories on your website that require password access and creating custom error pages that will be displayed when someone tries to access webpages on your site that do not exist. The features offered through a hosting company's control panel and the ease of its use are another consideration in selecting a service provider.

A fourth issue is adequate resources. Most hosting companies have multiple web hosting plans, with increased resources and software access in the more expensive plans. The resources usually include the amount of storage space on the server you will be allowed and the amount of material that can be downloaded from the server each month. Unless your journal is extremely successful, even the least expensive plans in most cases will provide adequate resources.

A fifth issue to consider is the software you will need to have available on the server. Any hosting company will have basic software, including web hosting, e-mail and software that supports file transfer protocol (FTP), the most common means of transferring files back and forth between the server and your personal computer. Depending on how you will be operating the journal, additional server software and features may be needed. This is a consideration, but it is quite possible that you will not know what you are going to need when starting a new journal. Fortunately, most hosting companies provide a substantial set of basic software, including programming languages, relational databases and other tools, although you may have to select a more expensive hosting option to get services such as access to a relational database. If you find you need something that is not provided by your plan, you may be able to get what you need by paying a little more for a higher-level plan rather than having to move to a different hosting company. It may be worth looking around at other hosting companies. In my experience, there are large differences not only in the amount of resources offered by different companies for roughly the same price but also in what software and options are offered in the least expensive hosting plans. If you have a limited budget, it can be worth the effort it takes to shop around for a hosting service. Some of the least expensive hosting companies offer excellent service and performance.

If you or your colleagues are comfortable developing your own webpages for the journal and plan on managing the peer-review process manually by using e-mail for manuscript submissions and communicating with your reviewers, you are likely to need little other than web hosting, e-mail support and access to FTP for file transfer from a hosting service. Most webpage development software, such as Adobe's Dreamweaver, supports FTP file transfer and can interface with the FTP software on the server to manage moving files back and forth between the developer's personal computer and the web server. Certain web development software, such as Microsoft's FrontPage and Adobe's ColdFusion, requires specialized software on the server to operate effectively. If you are planning on using these packages or others that require specialized software on the hosting server, it will be necessary to ensure the software is available. Most hosting companies support these products, though you may have to pay a little extra to access them.

Another software application that is often provided by hosting companies is a mailing list manager. Many electronic journals continue to bundle manuscripts into issues that are published at regular intervals. While this approach is necessary for paper journals for obvious logistical reasons, there is really no reason why manuscripts cannot be published in an electronic journal as they become ready for publication. In this situation, it is helpful to have a mailing list manager that allows interested readers to sign up to receive e-mail notices of newly published articles. With a mailing list manager this is easy to do and much appreciated by your readers. If you include the abstract and a link to the new articles your readers can simply 'click' on the link in the e-mail notice and access the article. The access to a mailing list manager is one of the software considerations in choosing a hosting company. Again, you may have to pay extra for this option with some companies.

If you will be using a journal management system (discussed in more detail below), and plan to install it on your own hosting account, it may be necessary to have additional software to support it. This is likely to include a server-side relational database manager and a server-side programming language. Fortunately, most hosting companies offer the software necessary for typical journal management systems. Once again, you may need to purchase a more expensive service plan in order to obtain access to the necessary software tools for the journal management software.

Changing web hosting companies

Fortunately, as long as you own the journal's domain name, it is a relatively simple process to switch hosting companies in such a way that it is completely transparent to your readers. Over the years, I have changed the hosting company used by *MEO* several times without problems. The best way to do this is to select a new hosting company before terminating your account with the old company. Set up the new hosting site without assigning your domain name to it. In most cases you should be able to access the site by using the IP address in place of a domain name, though with some hosting companies this cannot be done and you may have to purchase another domain name and use it temporarily to set up the site. Make an exact copy of your full journal site and upload it to the new server. Test it out very carefully to make sure everything works as it should. Every company's software and configuration are a little different, so you may have to make some adjustments to your journal website, but they should be minor. With both sites identical and everything working correctly on the new hosting site, work through the domain registrar where you purchased the domain name to transfer the name to the IP address of the new site. Sometimes this can be a little tricky, since there are safeguards to ensure domains are not fraudulently transferred, but the support people at the domain registrar should be able to help you through the process. Once the change has been implemented, it should ripple through the various name servers throughout the world and the people accessing your journal will begin accessing the new site as the name servers are updated. The process usually starts within an hour or two of the transfer being approved and completes within a day or two. Once the transfer is complete and you are sure the site on the new server is working correctly, you can close down the old server account.

Selecting a journal management system (or not)

Operating the peer-review and publication process manually is a reasonable way to run a small journal. As your journal grows, operating the peer-review process will become very labor-intensive. Journal management software specifically designed to streamline and track the peer-review process and other aspects of operating a scholarly journal will significantly reduce the effort required to run your journal. It will also allow you to keep much better track of manuscript submissions as they move through the review and publication process. This is critical, because as your journal grows you are likely to have a dozen or more manuscripts in various stages of the review/publication process and it is very easy for one to fall through the cracks until some frustrated author contacts you wondering what happened to their manuscript.

Although it is probably not necessary to use journal management software initially, I strongly suggest you consider implementing some type of this software when starting a new journal. This will avoid the need to make substantial changes to the way the journal runs while it is in operation, which causes confusion for you and everyone involved in your journal, including your reviewers and quite possibly the readers. Even though it may be some more work initially, you are likely to be better off in the end by implementing a system that will support the journal as it grows.

There are a number of journal management systems from which to choose. The SPARC publishing resources page (www.webcitation.org/5Mx98xweh) lists nearly 30 different journal management systems. Unfortunately, at the time of writing this chapter the list is somewhat outdated and a number of the links no longer work. It is, however, the only comprehensive list of journal management software I could find, and most of the listings are accurate and working.

Journal management systems vary in their capabilities, but typically they allow submission of manuscripts through a web form that collects the required information about the submission and uploads the manuscript to a server. Editors are notified by the system of new submissions and can select and assign reviewers via the web-based form after downloading and reviewing the submitted manuscript. Reviewers are usually notified by e-mail and can download review copies of the manuscript and complete their reviews online using web-based forms. Reviewer feedback is summarized for the editor, who can record the publication decision and respond back to the authors via the journal management software.

The real value of these systems is that they can automate virtually all the clerical work of distributing copies of manuscripts, collecting and collating reviews, contacting authors and reviewers and tracking each step of the process. The system lets you get a 'big picture' view of the review and revision process that can provide you with readily available statistics on the process and a better understanding of the flow of manuscripts through the system. You can also track the performance of your reviewers, replacing those who do not provide good feedback or are consistently tardy in returning reviews. Some systems go even further, managing the revision process, copy-editing and formatting and/or including tools that facilitate readers accessing the material. They also host the journal and avoid the need for you or your colleagues to do virtually any web development at all in managing the journal.

Most of these systems are owned and operated by commercial companies and are expensive, probably beyond the means of someone creating a new OA journal. But at least one excellent journal management system, Open Journal System (www.webcitation.org/5MvFe7h3e), is an open source project and can be downloaded and used at no cost. It is a full-featured system that will create and manage your whole journal website and can easily be customized so you can create a look and feel tailored to your own choosing. In my view, it is the best option for someone starting a new OA journal.

One disadvantage of OJS is that you must install and run it on your own server or web hosting account you obtain from a hosting company. It also requires Apache server software, the PHP programming language and one of two or three different relational database software packages – the most commonly used is MySQL. Fortunately these are widely used and most web hosting companies provide this software: it may mean purchasing a higher-cost hosting service in order to obtain access to the software, but many provide access to this software even for their least expensive hosting options. Installing OJS is very straightforward, and the Public Knowledge Project (www.webcitation.org/5MvErB1Hy) provides good documentation on the process. It requires no programming skills and the project has a bulletin board system where you can post questions and problems you have installing or using the software. They are usually answered within a few hours by one of the programmers who developed and maintain the software.

If you do not want to take on the task of locating and setting up the website and journal management software to start a new journal, another option is the Scholarly Exchange (www.webcitation.org/5QupAAhL5). The Scholarly Exchange runs OJS on its own server and provides access as well as full support for hosting OA journals. It does regular back-ups of the hosted journals, and takes care of managing the server. It will provide advice on setting up your journal website, letting you focus on running your journal. Use of the service is free for a new journal for one year. It does require that you allow context-appropriate advertising on the journal site to help defray the cost of the service. After one year there is a US$750 annual charge that is defrayed by half the revenue generated by the advertising on your journal website. This may well not cover the full cost of the yearly fee, but should generate at least some revenue and, as your journal becomes established, may actually provide some income beyond covering the hosting charge for funding other aspects of the journal.

The Scholarly Exchange is a good option if you do not have access to the technical expertise to manage your journal's web hosting and/or do not want to spend the time grappling with that aspect of publishing an OA journal. If you would prefer not to have advertising on your journal website, the Scholarly Exchange will provide the same service for US$1,000 per year, which is inexpensive compared with most commercial journal management systems. Also many of the commercial management services only handle the peer-review process, whereas OJS creates your whole journal website along with providing very useful tools facilitating readers accessing your material.

There are other options for journal management systems, and I suggest you spend at least a little time researching this issue. I suspect you will find, however, that OJS is the best option, and if you do not have the technical expertise or the interest in maintaining your own website, the Scholarly Exchange is a pain-free and inexpensive solution for hosting your journal.

Ensuring the availability and integrity of your journal

Back-up procedures

While paper journals by their very nature are extremely robust, unless specific steps are taken to ensure the safety of the contents of an electronic journal, they can be destroyed by a piece of faulty hardware or a careless mistake. As your journal grows, there is the potential of a real catastrophe if you do not set up some type of system to ensure the contents of your journal are protected. As stated above, when creating a scholarly journal, you have an obligation to both the authors who entrust you with their manuscripts and your scholarly field to protect the material contained in the journal.

You should ensure that back-up copies of all the key data related to the journal are made on a frequent and regular basis. Copies should be stored at multiple sites, since there is always a possibility of a fire or other disaster destroying all the material stored at a particular location. Key data include the published material, the journal website, correspondence and other records concerning submissions, and any material included in a journal management system if you are using one. If you do not back up regularly, almost invariably something important will get lost that will be difficult if not impossible to reconstruct.

Depending on who is hosting your journal, the web server support personnel may have an adequate system for back-up and recovery of the material on your journal website. But there is no guarantee this is the case, and you should investigate this issue rather than take it for granted. This is true whether your journal is hosted at your institution or through a commercial web hosting company. You should find out how often it is backed up, how long the back-up copies are kept, whether there are copies at multiple locations and how difficult or costly it will be to recover files. There are several potential problems that would require recovering lost material. These include hardware/software failures, disasters such as a fire, or an error on your part such as inadvertently erasing or corrupting key files.

When creating or updating websites, developers generally work on their personal computer and then upload finished webpages to the web hosting computer. This creates somewhat of a back-up system for your website, but in itself is probably not adequate. If whoever is maintaining the journal website inadvertently destroys or corrupts webpages or other files, it is likely that both the server and the copy on the personal computer where it was created will be corrupted. You or whoever is maintaining the journal website can implement a back-up of the site by ensuring a complete up-to-date copy or 'image' of the website from their personal computer is made on a regular basis. Using this approach will probably be necessary if you are obtaining your web hosting from a commercial company. In my experience they tend not to keep their back-ups for very long, and it can be difficult and/or possibly expensive to have the hosting company restore a copy of your site if you inadvertently destroy or corrupt some portion of it.

As noted above, you should ensure ancillary information related to the journal that is not stored on the server is also backed up regularly. How you accomplish this is up to you. Computer disk storage has dropped in price and continues to do so. External disk drives of several hundred gigabytes can be purchased for under US$100 today. Often you can find them with software specifically designed for back-up and recovery. Once configured, it can be as simple as pressing a button on the disk drive to back up the key files from the website as well as the directories on your computer with key information from the journal. Since it is a good idea to back up all your important digital information regularly, the back-up procedures for the journal can be incorporated into the general back-up of all your important information.

It is a good idea to have back-up copies at two locations. While rare, fires and other disasters occur, and recovering from them can be very painful or impossible without some planning. Given how easy and inexpensive it is to back up, keeping a second copy, for example at both work and home, just makes sense. With the price of miniature solid-state universal serial bus (USB) drives under US$50 for storage, these can serve as a convenient means of transferring regular back-up copies between locations.

There is no hard-and-fast rule on how often you back up and how long copies are kept. It is a question of balancing the cost and effort of the process versus the potential effort to re-create what is lost if there is some type of failure. As noted, many external disk drives come with software that makes backing up and subsequently restoring files very simple and convenient. They also generally provide options for incremental back-ups that only back up files which have changed or have been created in the interval since the last back-up, significantly reducing the amount of storage required. Backing up once a day is often a good choice, since it is easy to schedule and will avoid most serious losses of information. How you choose to design your back-up system is up to you, but have some reasonable set of procedures and follow them religiously.

Archival procedures

Back-up procedures can help ensure the content of your journal is not lost via an accident or disaster of some sort. But while essential for any electronic journal, they do not necessarily guarantee the contents of the journal will always be available, particularly if you are maintaining your journal by yourself or with the help of a small group of colleagues.

Maintaining the contents of a journal on the web takes some effort and expense. It is not much, but someone must attend to it. At some point we all retire, and as much as we would like to think otherwise, no one is immortal. Things change over time and there is no guarantee your new journal will continue into the future. You do, however, have an obligation to try to ensure the content of the journal remains available indefinitely. It is highly advisable to ensure copies of the journal's contents are contained in some type of archive maintained by a stable institution that you can be confident will be able to maintain the contents indefinitely.

One of the best solutions is LOCKSS, which stands for 'lots of copies keeps stuff safe'. Developed by Stanford University Libraries, LOCKSS (www.lockss.org/lockss/Home) is an open source application running on standard microcomputers that collects and stores digital content from the web. Many libraries participate in LOCKSS and have microcomputers running it. Using 'crawlers' similar to those used by search engines, they locate and archive the content of journals that have given their permission and been accepted by the libraries. The LOCKSS computers poll each other, make sure the content is consistent and resolve any errors. The multitude of computers each storing the contents of the journals in LOCKSS provides a highly automated and extremely robust archive that is available through any of the participating libraries.

While your journal may not be accepted by libraries immediately, once it becomes established you will probably have little trouble getting the content archived in LOCKSS. All you have to do is apply and provide a statement on your journal website giving the LOCKSS project permission to archive the content of your journal. The rest happens automatically. Once set up, LOCKSS will ensure the content of your journal is always available through the participating libraries.

Another potential archiving option is using an e-print archive. Many institutions are now setting up archives for electronic documents, including universities, professional organizations and governments among others. These archives contain digital written material, mainly journal articles, usually submitted by authors either prior to being published (pre-prints) or with the permission of the publisher after publication (post-prints). There are a growing number of these archives and at least some will archive the contents of journals.

If your institution maintains an e-print archive or you can identify one in your field of study that is well established and supported, it is worth investing the effort to get permission to add the contents of your journal to the archive. Your institutional librarian should be able to help you locate suitable e-print archives for your journal.

Not only will archiving the contents of your journal in an e-print archive help ensure the long-term availability of the contents, but it will probably help in wider dissemination of the contents. These archives often supply metadata to metadata harvesters (described in more detail in Chapter 7), which are searchable databases of digital content. This will provide another avenue for interested readers to locate material in the journal.

Well-known e-print archives that are included in major indexing services can be particularly powerful tools for both dissemination and ensuring the availability of content. Two excellent examples are PubMed Central, maintained by the US National Library of Medicine, and the Educational Resources Information Center (ERIC), maintained by the US Department of Education; these are archives that are connected to the most widely used indexes in their respective fields of biomedical research and educational research. Getting your journal included in archives such as these will dramatically increase the dissemination of your journal while ensuring long-term accessibility to the material.

By-laws, policies and other journal documentation

I strongly urge you to consider developing written by-laws, policies and instructions for authors prior to starting your journal. By-laws will help clarify how the journal will be organized and run, as well as who will perform various activities and how decisions concerning the journal will be made. While you may choose to publish your by-laws, they are mainly for internal consumption, defining how the journal will be operated. Written policies tend to be more externally focused, clarifying for authors, reviewers and readers the practices of the journal and expectations concerning issues such as copyright and how complaints will be handled and conflicts of interest addressed. Instructions for authors help contributors determine if their manuscripts are appropriate for the journal, and give requirements for style and format, how the manuscript should be submitted and policies and guidelines that must be met or followed for manuscripts to be considered for publication.

The nature of the by-laws and policies as well as the instructions for authors should reflect the type of journal you envision and the nature of your scholarly field. While there are no specific requirements for these documents, there are some general topics that should probably be addressed. Developing these documents will help you think through important issues that can easily be neglected among all the other activities necessary for getting the journal off the ground.

You will need to develop instructions for reviewers, as well as rating/feedback forms and associated documentation. It is also a good idea to develop an author agreement stating the intellectual property arrangement that allows the journal to publish the author's work, as well as assurances that the manuscript is the author's original work or that the author has obtained the necessary rights to include work owned by other parties.

By-laws

By-laws, as the term is used in this context, are rules adopted by an organization to govern its affairs. By-laws may not be necessary if you are creating a journal by yourself or possibly if you are developing the journal along with one or two close colleagues. If the journal will involve more than you alone, I would urge you to consider developing by-laws. Working through the process of developing the by-laws will help ensure the people involved in operating the journal have a consistent understanding of how it will function, how the various roles involved in operation are defined and the decision-making process for operating the journal. Developing by-laws will force you and your colleagues to discuss these issues up front and facilitate a clear understanding of who will do what and how the journal will function. Going through the process of making these decisions before the journal is in operation will help avoid conflicts down the road. Also, over time, the people involved in operating the journal are likely to change, and these by-laws will help provide an 'institutional' memory of the journal's practices.

By-laws set the foundation for the policies and procedures of an organization (Tesdahl, 2005). They define the structure of an organization and how it functions. By-laws are generally organized into sections in an outline style covering general topics, with a series of simple declarative sentences stating the organization and operation of the journal. Slaughter (2007) provides some suggestions for writing by-laws. The language should be clear and concise. Sentences should be structured so that it is impossible to quote provisions out of context. A standard format can help in avoiding repetition and facilitate locating specific provisions. By-laws need not be lengthy, nor detail the operation of the journal in very specific terms.

Some of the provisions you might consider in your by-laws include:

- name of the journal and a statement of its scope
- organization and personnel roles of the journal, including:
    - the editorial board's structure and function, and how members of the board are selected
    - the role and function of the editor(s) and how they are selected
    - listing of other journal staff roles and functions within the organization
- outline of the editorial/publication process
- schedule and description of the editorial board meetings or other regular meetings of the editorial team
- requirements and selection process for reviewers
- management and decision-making process for addressing financial issues
- process for amending the by-laws.

This is by no means an exhaustive list, nor are there specific provisions that are required. It is a good idea, however, to be sure to include a section on a process for amending the by-laws. You may find it helpful to review the by-laws of other journals to get an idea of the types of provisions that tend to be included and how they are written. Simply entering 'journal by-laws' into a web search engine such as Google will generate a long list of examples to review.

Policies

The distinction between by-laws and policies is a little murky. By-laws tend to be internal, codifying the structure, organization and operation of the journal. Policies tend to state practices, procedures or expectations for interactions between the journal and others such as readers and authors. Issues that are often addressed via a journal's policies include intellectual property rights and allowable uses for the contents of the journal, how conflicts and complaints will be addressed, requirements for manuscript submissions, such as expectations concerning the treatment of human and/or animal subjects in research submitted to the journal, and how potential conflicts of interest for authors, reviewers and editors should be addressed.

Whether you are operating your journal by yourself or with other colleagues, I strongly urge you to develop and post a set of journal policies on the journal's website. The specific nature of the policies is up to you, and should reflect the purpose of your journal and its nature and scope. While this is true, all journals should clearly state their policy on copyright ownership and acceptable use for the material in the journal. I also strongly advise you to include a policy for handling complaints concerning the journal's practices or material published by the journal. In most scholarly fields the potential for conflicts of interest exists, and it is advisable to include guidelines for how such conflicts should be disclosed or otherwise addressed. If the journal will be publishing research involving human or animal subjects it is also advisable to have a policy pertaining to the protection of human subjects and/or animals in research published in the journal.

As part of the submission process, you should also consider developing an author agreement that will serve as essentially a contract between the author and the journal. This agreement should state exactly what conditions and limitations authors grant for the material they are publishing through the journal. It should also include assurances from the authors, such as that the manuscript consists of original material or that they have obtained the necessary permissions for the inclusion of material for which they do not own the copyright.

The practice of requiring affirmation of an author agreement, usually in the form of a signed statement, is universal among traditional journals that require assigning to the journal copyright for articles published in the journal. It is less common among OA journals, where authors often retain copyright to their articles. I urge you to develop an author agreement and ask authors to affirm that they have read and accepted the terms of the agreement. If you are using an electronic submission system, this can be accomplished by requiring that they check a box saying they have read and accept the author agreement document, and have your software designed so as not to complete the submission process until the author has checked the box.

While OA journals often do not have a formal agreement that authors affirm, the same material is generally included in their instructions for authors. The advantage of having a formal agreement is that it helps avoid any ambiguity. The agreement clearly states the terms under which the journal will publish the authors' material, and the authors formally affirm that they have read and accept the agreement. In the vast majority of cases it is simply a formality; however, if a dispute arises over the terms of publication, it can be very helpful. The rest of this section discusses specific policies in more detail.

Copyright and acceptable use policies

Copyright laws vary from country to country, but most countries provide some type of protection to foreign works under certain conditions. There are two main international copyright conventions: the Berne Union for the Protection of Literary and Artistic Property (Berne Convention, www.web citation.org/5NvOefj9u), promulgated by the World Intellectual Property Organization, and the Universal Copyright Convention (www.webcitation.org/5NvOsYZY9). In drafting your policy you should also consider the laws governing copyright in your own country, although by their nature electronic journals are inherently international.

Traditionally scholarly journals have required authors to assign copyright for the material published in the journal to the journal's publisher in exchange for publishing the work. Publishers rationalized that this was necessary to be able to cover the costs of publication and protect the integrity of the authors' work. Scholars have begun to question the need for assigning copyright, and many if not most OA journals do not require that authors assign copyright for their work to the publisher. This is the case for all five journals described in Chapter 2.

An acceptable alternative is for authors to provide the journal with a limited license to distribute their work, outlining the acceptable use and conditions under which the material may be distributed. A very convenient and commonly used method for developing a license is through the Creative Commons (www.webcitation.org/5NyHV4PZn). The Creative Commons is a non-profit organization that provides a set of tools which intellectual property owners can use to develop licenses stating acceptable uses they wish to grant to others for their intellectual property. The Creative Commons offers six main licenses with different levels of restrictions on use.

Two of the five journals presented in Chapter 2, *IR* and the *JMIR*, use a specific Creative Commons license for defining the types of use allowed for the material they publish. *First Monday* allows authors to make their own decision on what types of uses are allowable and suggests authors consider using one of the Creative Commons licenses. This is an interesting approach and seems intuitively to be particularly fair and respectful of the fact that an author's work belongs to the author. My only concern with this approach is that it may be confusing to readers, who must check each article to determine the acceptable uses for the material it contains.

MEO has its own copyright policy that was developed by Georgia Harper, JD, who at the time was the senior attorney and manager of the Intellectual Property Section of the Office of General Counsel for the University of Texas System. It allows further distribution for non-profit purposes but requires specific permission from the author for other uses, such as repackaging or sale. I do not believe the Creative Commons licenses were available in 1996 when *MEO* was established, or at least I was not aware of them at the time.

One of the Creative Commons licenses is probably the best option for most new OA journals. They are very flexible and allow you to decide on the specific uses you feel comfortable allowing for the material in your journal. The language is very clear and the site provides a number of tools to facilitate the process. The licenses can also be tailored to the requirements of the specific laws of most countries, and they are widely used and accepted.

Along with specifying ownership and acceptable uses for the material contained within your new journal, your copyright policy should ask authors to affirm they own the material, or have obtained permission to use it, or the intellectual property that they do not own is in the public domain or their use of someone else's intellectual property clearly constitutes fair use. While your journal will probably still bear some responsibility if an author infringes on someone else's intellectual property, it is helpful to have a clear policy on the issue and to have required authors to assert that they have not infringed on someone else's intellectual property rights.

However you decide to define the acceptable uses of the intellectual material within your journal, it should be clearly specified on the journal website. Most people want to abide by the stipulations of the copyright owners, but this is obviously difficult to do if they are not clearly specified. While there is no guarantee that everyone accessing the material in the journal will abide by the requirements of the license, your best defense is to specify who owns the material and the acceptable uses.

Complaints policies

It is relatively uncommon for journals to have a complaints policy, but I have found *MEO*'s policy to be useful. There have been three formal complaints about the material contained within the journal over its 11-year history. Two were minor and easily resolved in ways that were acceptable to both parties. The third was a complaint of plagiarism, which was far more serious. *MEO*'s complaints policy was helpful in addressing the issue. When the complaint was received, I was able to reference it in explaining how the issue would be resolved. This I believe helped assure the author who made the complaint that it would be taken seriously. It also provided some general guidance for me in addressing the matter. Probably the most helpful aspect was having something to turn to in a situation that came as a real shock.

A complaints policy is no panacea, but it does provide a set of procedures and criteria in advance that can be followed to address the complaint. Developing a complaints policy before the need arises will allow you to focus on addressing the issues in the complaint rather than developing *ad hoc* procedures for addressing it.

How you wish to design your complaints policy and the level of detail at which to outline the procedures is up to you. *MEO*'s policy, which can be accessed on the journal's policy webpage (www.webcitation.org/5O62ATMD0), is very general, only asserting that complaints will be investigated by the journal and the broad criteria for removing material from the journal based on a complaint. It was developed by Georgia Harper, who developed all of *MEO*'s original policies.

Conflict of interest policy

Journal conflict of interest policies are becoming more common, particularly in the biomedical field. As the commercialization of research and scholarship grows, the concern about financial implications influencing, or at least having the appearance of influencing, research has increased.

There is nothing wrong or unethical about a conflict of interest. All of us have them. It is just that when your personal best interest may be affected by the results of research or scholarship that you have conducted, there is at least the appearance of potential bias.

MEO uses the following definition of a conflict of interest. 'A conflict of interest exists when an author's financial interests or other opportunities for tangible personal benefit may compromise, or reasonably appear to compromise, the independence of judgment in the research or scholarship presented in the manuscript submission.' Other journals have definitions that are more specific. They sometimes include precise monetary amounts for financial relationships, going above which constitutes a conflict of interest. While conflicts of interest are not necessarily financial, they are the most common and generally the main focus of conflict of interest policies.

There is a consensus that, in most cases, conflicts of interest are best handled by disclosure. Making readers aware of the conflict of interest allows them to make their own judgment about how to interpret the information presented in an article. If the scope of your journal includes research and scholarship that has the potential of involving conflicts of interest, and in particular financial conflicts of interest, it is probably best to have a stated conflict of interest policy that includes a requirement that authors disclose any potential conflicts of interest.

Use of animals and/or human subjects in research

Over the last half-century there has been a growing worldwide consensus on the need for rules governing the use of animal and human subjects in research. This is based on a history of widespread and egregious cruelty in the conduct of research involving both animal and human subjects. Many countries now have laws regulating the treatment of research subjects, and most journals that publish animal or human subject research have policies requiring authors to affirm that their research has complied with acceptable standards for its conduct.

What makes the process a little confusing is that there are a number of different definitions and standards, and different countries have different regulations and processes for ensuring guidelines are followed. If your journal will be publishing research involving animals and/or human subjects, I strongly suggest having a clearly stated policy requiring authors to affirm that the research has been carried out in a manner consistent with acceptable research practices for the use of animal and/or human subjects. One way to address the differences in laws and regulations among different countries is by requiring authors to affirm they have followed the regulations within the country in which the research was conducted. *MEO*'s text for human subject research is given below:

> Authors must confirm that they have followed all laws and regulations concerning the protections afforded human subjects in research studies within the jurisdiction in which a research study they describe was conducted. For research conducted within the United States, the research protocol must have been approved by the appropriate institutional review board (IRB). In the case of exempt research, the IRB must have deemed the research protocol exempt.

The additional language specific to the USA reflects the fact that, given the journal is based in the USA, approximately two-thirds of the manuscripts submitted are from the USA.

The *JMIR* addresses the use of human subjects by stating expectations for their treatment in research published in the journal. The following statement is contained in the instructions for authors:

> Internet-based research raises novel questions of ethics and human dignity. If human subjects are involved, informed consent, protection of privacy, and other human rights are further criteria against which the manuscript will be judged. Papers describing investigations on human subjects must include a statement that the study was approved by the institutional review board, in accordance with all applicable regulations, and that informed consent was obtained after the nature and possible consequences of the study were explained.

It also provides a number of references concerning ethical principles in human subject research.

The other three journals described in Chapter 2 do not have specific policies covering research on human or animal subjects. The scopes of these journals are such that human (or animal) subject research is less likely to be submitted as compared with *MEO* and the *JMIR*.

Policies concerning authorship

Another common journal policy concerns authorship. These policies generally seek to provide a clear definition of authorship and ensure all persons designated as authors qualify for authorship, and all those who qualify as authors are listed as authors. Policies also often seek to ensure that all the authors are familiar enough with the submitted manuscript to be able to take responsibility for it.

The criteria for authorship are generally that the person has made a substantive contribution to the manuscript or the research/scholarship on which it is based. Providing funding, supervision of the personnel working on the project and technical tasks such as copy-editing are generally not considered adequate contributions for being designated as an author; to qualify for authorship one must provide a significant intellectual contribution in conducting the research or scholarship, as well as drafting the manuscript. The 'Author and Contributor' section of the International Committee of Medical Journal Editors (ICMJE) *Uniform Requirements for Manuscripts Submitted to Biomedical Journals* (ICMJE, 2007) provides a good example of an authorship policy.

Policies concerning redundant publication

Many journals have specific policies that discourage duplicate or redundant publication. Not only will most journals refuse to publish duplicate or redundant manuscripts, but it is considered at least by some people to be scientific misconduct and is sometimes referred to as self-plagiarism. There are a number of different types of redundant publication, and the boundaries between what is considered appropriate and inappropriate are not entirely clear. Duplicate publication is generally defined as publishing exactly or essentially the same manuscript. A similar situation, sometimes referred to as 'salami slicing' (Roiq, 2007), consists of taking a single study or dataset and publishing multiple articles that are minor variations of the same study when it would be more reasonable to publish the information in a single article – an example would be publishing one article discussing gender differences based on a survey and another article discussing age differences based on the same survey.

Obviously there is a somewhat vague line between salami slicing and appropriately breaking up research results into multiple manuscripts when the results from a complex and/or rich dataset would be too cumbersome to describe in a single article. Also, there are situations when duplicate publication is justified. These are discussed in some detail in the *Uniform Requirements for Manuscripts Submitted to Biomedical Journals* (ICMJE, 2007) under the section titled 'Overlapping Publications'. One example is when a diverse audience would be interested in the information and publication in a single journal would not reach the entire audience. In such situations, one should inform the editors of each journal of what is being done and allow them to evaluate whether they feel it is appropriate to publish the manuscript.

Several concerns have been expressed about redundant publication. One of the most important ways scholars are evaluated is by the number of articles they publish and in which journals the articles are published. Redundant publication is seen by some as a form of cheating, allowing scholars to obtain multiple publications from what should be counted as a single publication. What role journals should have in terms of enforcing the appropriate review of scholars by their employers is a matter of debate. Secondly, and potentially much more serious from a scientific point of view, redundant publication, particularly duplicate publication, can bias research findings. Increasingly, multiple research studies are being aggregated in reviews of the literature. Particularly in the biomedical field, these aggregations are done using sophisticated statistical techniques under the rubric of meta-analysis. Whether the aggregation is done statistically or using less formal techniques, redundant publication, if not identified as such, has the potential of biasing the results of research reviews and meta-analyses on a particular topic by counting the same study multiple times.

How you decide to craft a redundant publication policy is up to you. You should, however, address this issue in some fashion, making it clear to authors what your expectations are in terms of manuscripts that could potentially be construed to be redundant publications.

Instructions for authors

Instructions for authors should clearly state the information authors need to decide whether their manuscript is appropriate for the journal, how to format the manuscript for submission, what other information is required for the submission and the policies the authors must comply with or agree to in order to have their manuscripts considered for publication. Instructions for authors should include the following (summarized in Table 5.1).

- A clear statement of the scope of the journal and the topics that are likely to be considered for publication.

- The acceptable formats and types of articles that are solicited, e.g. research, commentary, features, etc. This may include the approximate or maximum length and the typical sections that the manuscript should contain.

- Information on the style of writing, and conventions for organizing references, labeling tables and figures and other details on how the manuscript should be formatted. Specific areas of scholarship often have widely accepted guides for manuscript submissions. Examples include the *Uniform Requirements for Manuscripts Submitted to Biomedical Journals* (ICMJE, 2007) and the American Psychological Association publication manual (www.webcitation.org/5OKGF5KZo), which is widely used in the social sciences. Referencing a standard style guide that authors should follow greatly simplifies the process for everyone. If there is no standard style guide used in your area of scholarship, you might consider asking authors to follow a more general guide, such as the Chicago Manual of Style (2007).

■ Most manuscripts are submitted in electronic format. Be sure to indicate the acceptable digital format(s).

■ If your journal is published in HTML you may wish to request that authors submit their manuscripts in HTML or possibly plan text. It is helpful to have a HTML template they can download and use. The journal *Information Research*, described in Chapter 2, has used this strategy quite successfully. If you decide to accept word processing formats, Microsoft Word is a universal that virtually everyone either uses or can convert their manuscripts to. As with HTML, providing a template will simplify both the submission process for authors and the workload of your journal's staff or volunteers in formatting manuscripts for publication.

■ Specify how the material should be organized into digital files. Of specific concern is graphic material such as charts and figures. Left without directions, authors often embed their graphics files in the word processing document of their manuscript. It can be difficult to retrieve these graphics files out of the document in a format suitable for publication. It is best to have authors send them separately and specify the graphic file format(s) and resolution you require.

■ Be clear how you would like tables formatted and whether reference formats such as those generated by software like End Note are acceptable. I suggest asking authors to use the table creation feature available in word processors such as Microsoft Word. This again can save a great deal of effort preparing manuscripts for publication.

- Be specific and prescriptive in your formatting instructions. In my experience this can save many hours of tedious labor preparing manuscripts for publicaton. Authors often do not follow the instructions. I have found the best approach is to go ahead and send these manuscripts out for review if that is appropriate, but make it clear to the authors that they must revise the manuscript to meet your formatting requirements before it will be published. That way they do not have to put in the extra work to reformat the manuscript if it is not accepted. At the same time, we are very strict about authors following the manuscript submission formatting guidelines once a manuscript has been accepted, because it just means extra work for us if the guidelines are not followed.

- Clearly state the policies authors must agree to or affirm, such as copyright, redundant publication, authorship, conflicts of interest and/or use of animal or human subjects. If you are having authors submit manuscripts by e-mail, you can develop an author agreement form that they can sign and send digitally. Another strategy is to supply a statement affirming that they are complying with the policies of the journal and ask that it be included in the cover letter (e-mail) with the submission. If you are using an electronic submission system, you can include statements agreeing to or affirming compliance with the policies in the submission form and then use checkboxes for the authors to indicate their agreement.

- It is helpful for indexing purposes as well as assigning reviewers to ask authors to provide keywords describing their submission.

Table 5.1	Potential contents for instructions for authors

- Scope of the journal
- Article formats and other material considered for inclusion in the journal
- Detailed instructions on formatting style requirements for articles and other written material
- Review process and timeline
- Ownership and intellectual property requirements
- Policy issues
  - Human/animal protection requirements for research
  - Conflict of interest policy
  - Other policy issues or requirements related to submission material
- Submission procedures and forms
- Contact information for manuscript status, questions or concerns

Taking the time to develop detailed instructions for authors and carefully specifying your requirements will save you time and effort in the long run. This is particularly true for how submissions are formatted. Over time you may find you need to refine your instructions, particularly as you find more efficient ways to format manuscripts for publication. In addition, you will begin to learn the things authors do in formatting their manuscripts that inadvertently create a lot of work for the person reformatting them for publication. There is no reason to be hesitant in revising your instructions for authors and being very prescriptive in specifying the details of how manuscripts should be formatted when submitted for publication. While this may require a little more time and effort on the part of the authors who are submitting their manuscripts, once their manuscript has been accepted most authors are more than happy to comply with your requirements. Authors just have their own manuscript to address; you and your colleagues are tasked with formatting every manuscript that gets published, and the ten or

15 minutes of extra work per manuscript add up. Furthermore, if you are publishing an OA journal largely on volunteer labor, it seems quite reasonable to put the onus on the authors to do as much of the work as possible in formatting their manuscripts for publication.

Conclusions

Thinking through the process and developing by-laws, policies and submission instructions for your journal are important steps in its development. There are few hard-and-fast rules concerning what these documents should contain. They will, however, help shape your journal, and the process of developing them will help you think through the complex issues of creating a new journal as well as how it should be operated. I have tried to touch upon some of the important issues that may be addressed in these documents. The list is by no means exhaustive and will to a significant extent be shaped by your scholarly field and the nature of the journal you wish to create.

By-laws, policies and instructions for authors are not static documents, and it is certainly appropriate to modify and add to them over time. This will need to reflect your experience as well as changes in the scope and nature of the journal, and possibly changes in the expectations and norms of your scholarly field.

6

Resources and financing

Operating a journal takes resources. Until the development of the internet, only commercial publishers and scholarly societies could muster the resources necessary to publish scholarly journals. Additionally, the only practical way to fund journals was through subscription fees. With electronic publication and the use of the internet for communication, the resources required to publish a journal have dropped dramatically and it has become feasible for small groups of scholars or even single individuals to publish respectable peer-reviewed scholarly journals and not charge readers for accessing them.

Publishing a journal still takes resources, though not necessarily any cashflow. Garnering the necessary resources is likely to be one of your biggest challenges in creating and maintaining a new OA journal. Furthermore, the resources that will be required are not necessarily under your control, and are largely tied to the number of manuscript submissions the journal receives. As a new journal becomes established and submissions increase, it is possible to become overwhelmed by the resources and workload required for operating the journal.

This chapter will discuss strategies for addressing the challenge of obtaining the necessary resources to operate a new OA journal, as well as keeping from becoming overwhelmed as the journal becomes successful. There are a variety of strategies for obtaining resources. These were touched on in Chapter 2 in the description of the various types of OA journals. They encompass securing funding as well as obtaining volunteer effort. As noted, it is possible to operate an OA journal entirely on volunteer effort and donated web access, though I believe most OA journals have at least some limited cashflow. There are also a variety of ways to obtain operating funds, short of charging for accessing the journal. It is possible to charge for certain types of access such as PDF versions and still allow free access to less desirable formats such as HTML, or to ask authors to cover part of the cost of publishing their manuscripts. You may also be able to obtain donations or grants as a source of funding. As the journal becomes successful and a large number of people begin to access it, it may be possible to generate income through advertisements. There is no right or wrong way to secure funds, donated time and the other resources necessary to operate an OA journal. Every strategy has its advantages and disadvantages. Also, certain options may or may not be feasible given your specific situation. It comes down to a matter of the trade-offs among the various options that are available.

The five journals described in Chapter 2 reflect a variety of approaches to addressing the challenge of obtaining operating resources, and cover most of the available strategies. Each of these journals has addressed the challenge of resources somewhat differently, and will be used as examples of the types of trade-offs that have been made with the various strategies.

Reducing the need for resources by operating an OA journal efficiently

The more efficiently you can operate a journal, the less of a challenge obtaining the resources will be. Obtaining resources will always be difficult, so being as efficient as possible is probably the most effective strategy to use in addressing the resource issue. Electronic communication technology is a powerful means of increasing efficiency. Moving the publication process on to the web has made OA journals possible. Moving the peer-review process and other journal management tasks on to the web dramatically reduces the workload of operating the journal. Just conducting the peer-review and revision process using e-mail removes the costs of copying and mailing. It also significantly reduces the workload of conducting peer review and revision of manuscripts.

The up-front work of setting a journal management system up will be well worth the effort in the long run, and systems like OJS are available at no cost. Taking advantage of technology to the maximum extent possible is likely to be your most effective means of reducing the cost and effort required to operate a new OA journal and address the daunting challenge of continuing to maintain the journal as it becomes successful and the workload of operating it begins to increase exponentially.

As a journal grows, the task of the editor can become overwhelming. An efficient way to address this is to implement a hierarchical review system with managing editor(s) and multiple review editors. The different review editors may also each focus on different areas or sections within the scope of the journal. This is a very effective way to spread editorial workload over a number of individuals and keep workload manageable for each editor, particularly when those editors are working for the journal on a volunteer basis. Many journal management programs such as OJS support a hierarchical review system.

MEO operates with such a system, and we have found it to work quite well. As manuscripts are received, one of the managing editors performs an initial review. If the manuscript does not fall within the scope of the journal or is clearly not publishable, the managing editor rejects it at that point and informs the author of the rejection and reasons for rejecting the manuscript. Otherwise the managing editor assigns the manuscript to one of six review editors, who prepares the manuscript for publication and manages the review and revision process from that point on.

Volunteer help

Most OA journals run to some extent on volunteer labor and donated support. As noted above, most of the clerical aspects of operating an electronic journal can be automated through server-based journal management software. What remains includes the editorial tasks of reviewing submissions, managing the peer-review process and responding back to authors summarizing the results and making a publication decision. Working with authors on the revision process can take a significant amount of effort. Once the journal becomes established, responding to e-mail correspondence can also take a significant amount of time.

Along with the editorial tasks there are copy-editing, formatting manuscripts for publication and potentially web maintenance. You may also need to create XML or other records for indexing and archiving manuscripts. Depending on the nature of the journal there may be a substantial amount of administrative work required to maintain the journal. This might include planning meetings and record-keeping. During the development phase, creating forms, procedures and documentation is likely to require a considerable amount of effort. If the journal has a significant budget, there are accounting and tax issues. If services such as copy-editing and web development are contracted out or individuals are hired by the journal, the administrative aspects of supervising employees or managing contractors can be substantial.

I have found garnering help to perform these tasks much more difficult than finding willing volunteers to perform the editorial and review functions of a journal. University faculty are encouraged to undertake editorial work and rewarded for it. This makes it relatively easy to find faculty who are willing to help in these roles, and if you implement a hierarchical review system with multiple review editors, the workload for each editor can be kept at a reasonable level. Tasks such as the copy-editing, formatting and web design and maintenance are a different story. They take significant technical skill. These tasks are generally not viewed as scholarly work and provide faculty with little credit for promotion and tenure. Additionally most faculty are not skilled in these technical areas. While it is not difficult to find people who have these skills and are willing to take on these tasks, in most cases they expect to be paid and the per-hour charges are expensive. It is not impossible to find people willing to perform these tasks on a volunteer basis, but it will be very difficult.

One strategy we are currently exploring with *MEO* is the use of graduate student interns. We recently had a graduate student in English who was interested in electronic journals participating in a semester-long internship. We are currently working to formalize and expand the program so it can be made available to students at other institutions. I believe both undergraduate and graduate student internships have the potential to be a very valuable source of volunteer labor. Developing an internship program will require some effort to create a reasonable structure for the program and supervise the students. In most cases there should be a net time advantage, with students accomplishing far more than the effort it takes to supervise and teach them. Furthermore, faculty are likely to receive some academic credit for developing and operating an internship program. Not only can this experience be valuable for the journal, but it is also a great opportunity for the students to learn about the value of OA journals.

Authors are also a source of volunteer labor that can significantly reduce the workload of preparing manuscripts for publication. This was discussed to some extent in the last chapter on developing instructions for authors. Carefully specifying how manuscripts should be formatted when submitted for publication is a simple and effective way of reducing your workload. In my experience, manuscripts are most often submitted in Microsoft Word format. Word allows the creation of templates where formats for specific sections of the documents, such as titles, references and various levels of headings, can be specified and selected from pull-down menus. Providing a template and insisting authors use it simplifies the process for them and helps ensure manuscripts are received in a consistent format.

A reasonable compromise that makes life easier for authors while simplifying the preparation of manuscripts is to be flexible in terms of the format in which manuscripts are received for review. At *MEO* we accept manuscripts in any reasonable format that our reviewers can easily read. We insist, however, that the manuscripts adhere to our specified submission format prior to being accepted for publication. Since manuscripts are often submitted to more than one journal before they are accepted and published, this saves authors the work of reformatting their manuscripts only to find they have not be accepted. Once accepted, authors tend to be more than happy to reformat their manuscripts to our specifications.

Another strategy that can significantly reduce costs and effort is to forgo copy-editing by the journal and put the onus on authors to ensure their manuscripts are well written and suitable for publication when submitted in their final form. Although this may seem radical, it is the policy of many of the BioMed Central (BMC) journals. Despite this policy, these journals are receiving growing respect and some are beginning to have very impressive impact factors.

Electronic journals by nature are very international and you are likely to receive manuscripts from all over the world. Authors whose primary language is not the language in which your journal is published will generally need significant help editing their papers. In our experience at *MEO*, even the papers from authors from other English-speaking nations generally need additional editing to be consistent with *MEO*'s style. I suspect wherever your journal is located and whatever language will be used in publication, you will face the need to provide some level of copy-editing to ensure the journal has a consistent style.

Donated support

Many OA journals rely heavily on donated support in the form of resources, technical expertise/effort and funding. All of the journal examples in Chapter 2 have had some donated support and three of these, *First Monday*, *IR* and the *JEP*, receive significant donated support. One of the most common sources of support is university libraries; in fact more and more libraries are providing integrated publishing systems and support for journals and other material published by faculty in their institutions. A good example is the University of Michigan University Library Scholarly Publishing Office (http://spo.umdl.umich.edu/), which publishes the *JEP*. In addition, the University of Illinois at Chicago Library provides technical support for *First Monday*, Lund University Libraries provides technical support for *IR* and the Swedish School of Library and Information Science provides some editorial support as well.

It is not surprising that university libraries are a common source of support for OA journals. In my experience there is no group more aware of the issues facing scholarly publishing or more supportive of OA as a solution for many of these problems than librarians. Not only are academic libraries as organizations and librarians as professionals supportive of OA publishing, but their area of expertise is relevant and they tend to possess important technical skills that are very useful in publishing an OA journal. Your institution's library would be a good place to begin when seeking resources to launch a new OA journal. Beyond the library, you may be able to obtain support from your institution. Journals bring significant prestige and enhance the reputation of a university or other organization and, in the case of electronic journals, do not necessarily cost a great deal. At a minimum, you may be able to acquire some protected time to work on the journal as well as web server access and support.

Foundations are another potential source of support. The Open Society Institute (www.webcitation.org/5OmRYAx2h) has funded various OA projects, including at one point the publication costs of authors from developing countries submitting manuscripts to the *JMIR*. While the Open Society Institute does not appear to be providing general funding for OA journals, you may be able to identify foundations that have a particular interest in the material published by your journal or possibly a smaller local foundation that would be receptive to providing support. There are a number of searchable databases of foundations, and the research office at your institution can help identifying potential sources of support.

Seeking grant support from a foundation or other entities has several potential disadvantages. First, it takes a lot of time to identify potential sources and write proposals requesting funding, and there is no guarantee of success. The effort it takes to develop proposals is effort that could have gone into other aspects of operating the journal. Administering a grant once one is received also takes time and effort, again detracting from the time available for working on the journal. While it possible to obtain continuing support from foundations, they often prefer to provide funding to get projects off the ground, making it even more difficult to find the continuing funding to maintain a journal.

It is sometimes possible to obtain funding through corporate sponsorship. The *JEP* has been very successful in this venue and currently has ten sponsors. Accepting funding of this sort requires a delicate balance, and one runs the potential risk of at least the perception of conflict of interest and bias. Before embarking on this route, I suggest thinking very carefully about the implications for your journal's reputation.

Another potential source of resources for publishing an OA journal is the government. A growing number of governments have realized the value of OA journals and are providing support for scholarly journals. A good example is the Scientific Electronic Library Online (SciELO, www.webcitation.org/5P3BP4aXp), which is a model for cooperative electronic publishing in developing countries, based in Brazil.

Generating income through the journal's operations

Many OA journals generate at least part of their operating expenses from their operations, but still make the content freely available in some form. A number of these funding models were mentioned in Chapter 2. This section will discuss several strategies for generating income from the operation of a journal while still providing journal articles in some form at no charge.

Author-fee models

The most common method of generating income from an OA journal's operations is to charge authors for publication. While the majority of journals that use this model only charge authors when their manuscripts are accepted for publication, some journals charge submission fees as well. Fortunately, many funding agencies consider these charges a legitimate expense for publishing the results of grant-funded research, easing the burden on authors who are fortunate enough to have grants from an agency willing to pay publication fees. Paying publication fees, which can be quite expensive, is a real issue for many authors, particularly those from developing countries. Some publishers waive the fees for authors from developing countries and/or authors who can demonstrate that paying the fees would be a significant hardship. BioMed Central is an example of a publisher which charges publication fees but waives those fees for authors from developing countries. While this partially mitigates the problem, I feel this strategy has real drawbacks as well as some distinct advantages.

My major concern is that it discourages if not precludes some authors from publishing in an OA journal. There is a growing understanding in academia of the crisis in scholarly publishing and the benefits of OA publishing. It is, however, very easy to rationalize submitting an article to a pay-for-access journal in lieu of paying a publication fee that can run into thousands of dollars, particularly when it is coming out of one's own pocket. While many of the journals that charge author fees have been successful, I suspect the fees discourage some authors from submitting their manuscripts to one of these journals.

The use of author fees does have significant advantages. It is the simplest and most straightforward way to provide open access and generate the funding necessary to operate a journal on a truly professional level. While it is possible to operate an OA journal on almost no funding, finding resources for copy-editing, formatting, indexing and web development is a challenge and I suspect in most cases these journals are not professionally edited and formatted and tend not to have the same level of indexing and archiving found in professionally published journals. Charging author publication fees can level the playing field, allowing the creation of journals that do not charge for access but are every bit as polished as commercial or society-published journals that charge subscription fees. This is not to say journals that operate on little or no funding cannot be excellent journals. It just that they tend to lack the same 'polish' and professional appearance of journals with the budgets to hire professionals to do the copy-editing, formatting and web development.

The other advantage of charging author fees is that the income generated is consistent with the number of manuscripts published. Since the cost and effort of operating the journal closely parallel the material published, this helps ensure there are adequate resources to meet the increasing needs of a journal even when it grows rapidly.

Charging for added-value products

It is also possible to generate income by charging for 'added-value' products such as PDF-formatted articles. This is attractive, in that it provides open access to the content of the journal for anyone who wishes to access it, and at the same time can generate income by charging readers who are willing to pay for higher-quality formats, bundled article collections or other enhancements to the basic material. Among the journals discussed in Chapter 2, the *JMIR* uses this strategy to generate part of its operating funds. Another example of a well-known journal that uses this strategy is *Postgraduate Medicine*.

This model assumes that there will be people willing to pay for these added-value products or formats. It is not clear that this is always the case, nor how much income can be generated through this strategy. However, the strategy does provide a means of generating income while allowing open access without having to resort to author fees.

Advertising

A third way to generate income from the operation of an OA journal is through advertising on the journal's website. Advertisers such as Google have designed systems that sense the type of content contained on a website and display advertising that is relevant and appropriate for the site. These are usually displayed in banners or boxes in various locations on the webpages on the site. The systems are easy to set up and in my experience quite effective in supplying appropriate advertising content that is likely to be of interest and not offensive to the readers. You also have control over on which pages and where on the page the advertisements appear.

Probably the most widely used system of this type is Google Adsense, but there are a variety of other advertisers. Google also has a search engine option where you can display a Google search box that can limit searches to just the journal or the web as a whole. When the search box is used by someone accessing the journal, they get relevant advertising links along with the links generated by the search, and you receive payments for 'clicks' on the advertised links.

There are a whole variety of other website advertising models, but the one above is a good option if you choose to use advertising as a means of generating operating expenses for your journal. Since the material is targeted to the site it can be helpful to your readers and there is an increased likelihood that they will 'click' on an advertising link, generating income. Since you have control over on which pages and at what locations on a page the advertisements appear, as well as the color scheme of the advertisements, it is possible to design them to fit well and not detract from the aesthetics of the journal.

Advertising is an attractive means of generating funds for operating the journal. It is simple and easy to implement and requires very little maintenance. It does not cost your readers or authors anything, and can be potentially useful to the readers in locating products or services they are likely to be interested in exploring. The disadvantages of advertising are that it is unlikely to generate a significant amount of income and some people may feel it detracts from the academic/professional nature of the journal.

Of the five journals described in Chapter 2, *IR* and *MEO* use this type of advertising to generate income and the *JMIR* has used it in the past. At *MEO* we decided to add Google Adsense in hopes of generating enough income to provide for professional copy-editing, along with covering the costs of the commercial internet service provider hosting the website. While the income that is being generated is more than adequate for covering the costs of hosting the journal, it has not been enough to pay for professional copy-editing. Part of the reason is that *MEO* manuscripts are published as

PDF files and a high percentage of the connections to our site go directly to the PDF copies of the manuscripts, bypassing any advertisements.

The amount of income that advertising will generate is closely tied to the amount of traffic on the journal site and roughly tied to the number of submissions and articles published on the site, which largely determine the resources needed for copy-editing, formatting and web maintenance. It is unlikely that advertising on your journal site will provide the necessary income for professional copy-editing, formatting, indexing and web development/maintenance, but it can generate a steady income stream and help defray the costs of operating the journal.

Administrative overhead

One of the problems with generating income for operating a journal is that it creates administrative overhead. In general, the more income you are able to generate from a variety of sources and the more heavily you rely on employees or paid contractors to perform various functions of the journal, the more time and effort someone will have to expend on administrative tasks. Generating income requires implementing and performing accounting procedures as well as addressing the tax issues. Obtaining donations through grants and sponsorships can take a great deal of effort as well, with no guarantee of success, and once funding is obtained there usually is a fair amount of work tracking expenses, keeping records and filing reports. Contracting for services also requires administrative overhead, and hiring employees is even more time-consuming. In essence, the more cashflow you are able to generate and the more of the work required to operate the journal is done for pay, the more effort it will take to oversee and administer the process, which detracts from the time you and your colleagues who started the journal can put towards the tasks of actually operating the journal. This is not to say you cannot reduce the workload of operating an OA journal by generating income and hiring professionals to perform the technical tasks of operating the journal. It is just that the larger the operation, the more time someone will have to spend on the ancillary tasks involved in generating income as well as acquiring and overseeing professional help in operating the journal.

Conclusions

There is neither an easy solution nor a single strategy for obtaining the necessary resources to publish an OA journal. Obtaining resources is a constant struggle for most OA journals. It certainly has been the case for *MEO*. Using the internet and journal management software to operate your journal as efficiently as possible is a very effective strategy for reducing the workload. The decision on whether to attempt to generate income or rely largely if not entirely on volunteer effort is difficult. It is possible to operate a very respectable OA journal largely on volunteer effort alone, with virtually no external resources, by keeping the operation very lean and relying on the authors to take responsibility for much of the copy-editing and formatting effort for their manuscripts. *MEO*, *IR* and *First Monday* have largely chosen this route, though each has some external support and provides some level of copy-editing and formatting for the material it contains. It is very difficult, however, to achieve the same level of quality and sophistication with volunteers as compared to using professionals. This is not to say you cannot create an excellent, highly respected journal on volunteer effort alone.

It just is unlikely to have the same polish as a journal operated by professionals.

The *JEP* and *JMIR* have each taken a different approach to addressing the resource issue. The *JEP* has been very successful in obtaining donated support. It is currently operated by the Scholarly Publishing Office of the University of Michigan Library and has numerous corporate sponsors. The *JMIR* generates a significant portion of its operating expenses through its operations, using a variety of different mechanisms. Authors are charged both submission and publication fees. The journal charges for added-value products such as PDF versions of the manuscripts and compilations of articles in PDF format. It also seeks funding from sponsors in exchange for access to its added-value products and waivers of fees for publication. Despite charging submission and publication fees, the journal has been very successful in attracting submissions. The significant cashflow the *JMIR* receives has allowed it to have full-time employees and operate on a more professional basis than would likely be possible with volunteer help alone.

As stated at the beginning of this chapter, there is no easy answer or correct way to address the challenges of providing the necessary resources to publish an OA journal. Each strategy and source of income and resources has its strengths and limitations.

7

Disseminating the content of your journal

Indexing is the most effective means by which you can integrate the content of your new journal into the body of literature in its field and ensure that the journal content can be easily located by scholars. Getting a new journal into major indexes is very challenging and may not be possible initially. We will discuss a number of other strategies for disseminating the content of your new journal and helping ensure that the people interested in your area of scholarship can easily find relevant material in your journal.

Obtaining an International Standard Serial Number

The ISSN (International Standard Serial Number) identifies periodical publications as such (ISSN International Centre, 2007). An ISSN is an eight-digit number (two groups of four digits separated by a hyphen) that provides a uniform worldwide system for identifying serial publications. Serial publications, which include scholarly journals, are 'publications, in any medium, issued in successive parts, usually having numerical or chronological designations and intended to be continued with no predetermined end' (ISSN International

Centre, 2007). With tens of thousands of journals, having a worldwide standard labeling convention is immensely helpful for libraries, journal indexes, publishers and others who must work with large numbers of different publications.

Getting an ISSN number assigned to your journal is a relatively simple matter and there is no cost involved. This is something you should definitely do when starting a new journal. There is an international center based in Paris that coordinates 83 national centers. The international center has a listing of the national centers (www.webcitation.org/ 5Pgj3o8WZ), from which you can find the appropriate center to apply for your journal's ISSN. If your country does not have a center, you should contact the international center. It is possible to apply prior to launching the journal, but it is a good idea to wait until you are able to supply most of the requested information. You just have to complete a form to apply for and obtain an ISSN number for your journal.

Indexes

No one knows exactly how many peer-reviewed scholarly journals are currently being published, but the number is clearly in the tens of thousands. The most common way scholars are able find the material they need when there are dozens or even hundreds of relevant journals is through the use of journal indexes. These indexes provide searchable metadata (data about data), including abstracts from the contents of hundreds and in some cases thousands of different journals. They are extremely helpful in conducting efficient and comprehensive searches of the literature on a topic. Some indexes are owned by commercial companies, others are owned by scholarly societies. These are largely funded by subscription fees from academic libraries. There are also publicly funded indexes, such as the National Library of Medicine's Medline that covers biomedical fields and the US Department of Education's Educational Resources Information Center (ERIC) that covers education.

Getting your journal included in the major indexes that cover the scope of the journal will greatly enhance the ability of readers to find the content in your journal. Not only will this facilitate scholars in the field accessing the information contained in the journal, but it is a sign that your journal is recognized as a high-quality, well-established journal. While being added to the major indexes in your field is an important goal, it is also a challenge for a new journal with limited resources and a lack of a record of accomplishment in publishing quality scholarly research. In most cases, indexes will not automatically index a new journal. There are considerable costs and effort involved in the process, since the indexing is done manually by professional indexers. Each indexing service has criteria and some sort of review process for adding new journals into the index. At the same time, it is in the index's interest to index important journals in the field(s) it covers (Stranack, 2006).

The first step you should take is to identify the appropriate indexes for your journal. Indexes vary in scope. Some are very broad and index journals in a wide variety of fields – an example is Thompson's Web of Science. Other indexes cover a general area, for example Wilson Social Sciences Index, and some indexes focus on a specific field, such as PsycINFO. As a scholar or scientist you are probably familiar with at least the major indexes in your field of study. It also makes sense to try to identify additional indexes with which you may not be familiar. A good source of information is your institutional library. The librarian who handles your scholarly field should be able to provide you with advice on what indexes to explore.

Once you have identified the indexes you would like to pursue, locate their websites, which should contain a section on information for publishers. This section will have the criteria for inclusion, a description of the review process and information on how to get your journal reviewed.

Since an established record of publishing quality articles is one of the major criteria for most indexes, getting your journal into the key indexes in the field may not be possible for some time after the journal's launch. Many indexes also require a waiting period of several years before a journal can reapply for inclusion after being rejected. With this in mind, you should carefully consider whether it would be better to wait for your journal to become more established before applying for inclusion in a major index.

Fortunately there are a variety of other strategies for disseminating information about your journal and getting located by scholars who are interested in its scope.

Directories

Directories of journals can be useful in making the content or at least the existence of your journal known to likely readers. As noted above, indexes generally use professionals to index articles, which is a time-consuming and expensive process. Directories of journals tend to be much less selective, since they do not use professional indexers. There are dozens of such directories. Like indexes, some cover a wide variety of fields and some focus on a specific area of scholarship. Most can be accessed without restrictions. Many just list journals and their URLs, but others include information describing the journal and some even include article-level metadata. Two examples of broad-based directories are 'New Jour' and ejournals@cambridge.

One of the most relevant directories, and one in which you should definitely list your journal, is the Directory of Open Access Journals (DOAJ), developed and maintained by Lund University Libraries (www.webcitation.org/5SdGZMgV0). The directory contains full-text, open access scientific and scholarly journals that use an appropriate quality control system to guarantee the content of the journal. Journals are required not to have any embargo period. The DOAJ lists at the time of this writing more than 2,700 journals and maintains article-level metadata if journals are willing to submit the information.

Another important directory is the Open Directory Project (ODP, www.webcitation.org/5PRiC89eb). The ODP is probably the most comprehensive human-edited directory of the web. It contains far more than just journals, but is definitely a site where you should submit your journal. The ODP is maintained by over 75,000 volunteers who review, select and index websites. Not only is the ODP widely used but, since it is indexed by volunteers who have some expertise in the areas they index, your site will probably be appropriately categorized. Another good reason for submitting your site is that the ODP is used by some major search engines, such as Google, as a source for their own automated indexing activities.

Making sure your journal is listed in as many of the relevant directories as possible will help in dissemination. Search engines (discussed below) also use the number of links from highly accessed and relevant sites as a key criterion in ordering the results of their search. Having your journal listed in major directories will help in improving search engine ranking, generating more traffic to your journal indirectly via search engines as well as directly from people finding it in the directory.

In most cases, getting into a directory is just a matter of filling out a form. The librarians at your institution can help you locate appropriate directories for your journal. You can also find them by searching on the web. Many libraries have lists of directories that are often made available on their websites. With the help of your librarian and some detective work, you should be able to locate the major directories covering the scope of your journal and determine how to get your journal added to each of these directories.

Metadata harvesters

Metadata harvesters are software programs that harvest metadata describing the contents of a repository containing digital resources. The harvested metadata records are generally organized into a searchable database which can be used to facilitate finding resources located in the repositories that have been harvested. These harvesters are often operated by university libraries.

Metadata are simply data describing data. There are formalized and systematic procedures for creating the type of metadata accessed by harvesters. By creating a systematic set of data describing the contents of an archive, such as the articles in an OA journal website, and providing harvesters with the location of the metadata file, the harvester can gather and incorporate the metadata into a searchable database describing the contents of the journal or other archive. Like an index, scholars can use the database to search a large number of archives efficiently for material on a specific topic. Creating metadata for the contents of your new journal and registering them with a number of harvesters is another strategy that you can use to disseminate the material in the journal.

Since the harvesting process is automated, the metadata need be organized in a systematic format or protocol. Probably the most commonly used metadata harvesting protocol is the

Open Archives Initiative Protocol for Metadata Harvesting (www.webcitation.org/5PK1UEHnz). This outlines both the required format for the metadata in the archive and the protocol for harvesting them.

Part of the metadata for the records of the material in your journal will be consistent across all the material in the journal, or at least for a section of the journal. Examples include copyright/rights management information, the language in which it is published and the publisher. Much of the rest of the metadata will describe the article. Most of these can be captured from the author during the submission process. Examples include author information, title, keywords and an abstract. Additional information is set at the time of publication, such as the date of publication, issue/volume and the location of the manuscript.

It is possible to create a template with the information in the correct format that only requires someone to fill in the unique information for each article's metadata record. This is a workable but tedious and time-consuming process that will have to be done for each article or other manuscript published. Fortunately journal management software already collects most of the necessary information and can be designed to generate metadata records as articles or other material are published, automating the process of creating metadata. If you will be using OJS, it has the ability to create metadata consistent with the Open Archives Initiative protocol. If you are not using OJS or some other journal management system capable of generating its own metadata, your institution's library can help you to develop a procedure for creating metadata describing the contents of your journal in the appropriate format for them to be harvested, and to get the journal registered with key harvesters.

One of the best-known harvesters is OAIster (www.oaister .org/), maintained by the University of Michigan. There are many others. Again, your institution's librarian can help you identify the more relevant harvesters for your journal.

Search engines

Search engines such as Google, Yahoo! and Ask are another means of advertising your journal and its contents. Search engines automate the process of identifying and indexing content. They use computer programs called 'bots' or 'spiders' to 'crawl' the web, jumping from link to link gathering huge searchable databases that contain text from millions and millions of webpages. Google is probably the best known, but there are many others search engines.

A growing number of scholars are using search engines to locate resources in their academic fields. I have found these search engines to be a significant source of referrals to *MEO*. For example, in the week prior to writing this chapter, *MEO* received over 2,000 referrals from search engines.

There are both general search engines, such as the three mentioned above, that index the web broadly and search engines that just cover specific types of content. Google Scholar focuses on scholarly content and, obviously, is one you should ensure indexes your journal. Other focused search engines may also be relevant to the scope of your journal. Your institution's librarian can help you identify the most appropriate search engines for your particular field.

It is relatively easy to have your site indexed by these search engines. The challenge is to be near the top of the list in the results for searches that are relevant to your journal. Given the tremendous amount of material on the web, when queried search engines often generate lists of thousands or even millions of webpages that meet the search criteria. People using a search engine rarely go beyond the first dozen or so entries on a list of results, and it is not much help to have the articles in your journal site listed a few thousand entries down from the top. Search engines use complex algorithms for ordering search results, with the goal of placing the most relevant material at the top of the results. While the specifics of the algorithms used by each search engine are trade secrets, there are general guidelines that can be helpful in raising your site's ranking in searches. Additionally, most search engine companies provide specific guidelines for ranking well on their searches.

You can run afoul with search engines by using what search engine operators feel are devious techniques to try to increase the rank of the journal's webpages on their searches. These are usually pretty obvious and easy to avoid, like plastering your site with hundreds of search terms in text and then hiding these from your viewers by making the foreground and background colors the same. The search companies do check for things like that as they 'crawl' the web, and will stop listing your site altogether if they feel you are using inappropriate techniques to raise your rankings.

You should submit your site to the major search engines and any specialized search engines that are relevant to the scope of your journal. While the search engines are likely to find your site on their own eventually, submitting your site should speed up the process of getting your site indexed. You actually do not have to submit your site to each search engine, since many of the search engines have agreements where they share information. These relationships are constantly changing, but Bruce Clay Inc. (www.webcitation .org/5PfnOtqQ2) has a very nice interactive chart that shows the current relationships. From the chart, you can determine to which search engines you will need to submit your site to cover the majority of the major search engines. This is also an excellent site to learn more about search engine optimization, discussed below. Most search engines have a section for web developers that provides you with information on how to submit your site. If you go to the main site for a particular search engine, you should easily be able find how to submit your site.

There are strategies that can improve your site's rankings for relevant search queries. This is termed search engine optimization (SEO). Before discussing these, it is important to realize that obtaining the top rankings on search engines is a topic that has huge implications for the thousands of companies that do business or advertise their services through websites. For this reason, SEO has become a professional field in its own right, with consulting companies, websites devoted to the issue and even its own professional organization. There is an interesting dynamic between the search engine companies that strive to ensure their searches provide the most relevant websites at the top of their search lists and a whole professional field dedicated to devising strategies to place their clients' webpages as high as possible in the search order for keywords and phrases relevant for their products. The net result is that both the algorithms used by the search engines and the strategies used to improve rankings are constantly changing.

While keeping up with the professionals whose careers are based on obtaining high search rankings for their clients is neither practical nor necessary, there are things you can do to improve the search rankings for your journal articles. There are numerous websites focused on how to improve rankings. SearchEngineWatch.com (www.webcitation.org/ 5PXV1t22c) is a very good site with a nice introductory tutorial. The tutorial is free, but you have to become a paid member to receive the best information. SEMPRO (www .webcitation.org/5PWP3AQYz), the professional organization of the search engine marketing industry, is another good site with useful content. Bruce Clay's site, discussed above, is a good source of information. It may be worth devoting half an hour to going through the SearchEngineWatch.com tutorial, but it is probably not worth spending any more time than that on learning about search engine optimization, unless of course you are interested in the topic.

One simple thing you can do is to include an HTML title and meta-'description' element for each webpage you would like to have highly ranked in searches, and carefully choose the text for these commands. The 'head' section of an HTML webpage contains information that describes the HTML page (www.webcitation.org/5PWHPRuTK). The title contains a short description of the material contained in the webpage. The 'head' section can also contain 'meta'-statements that specify a name (specifies the type of information) and value (descriptive information) about the page. The 'description' meta-statement is used to provide a brief description of the page.

Most search engines index the text in the title and description meta-statements on a page. They also may be used to create the short description of the site that most search engines provide with the name and link in the search results. Search engines also index the text contained in the body of a webpage, and in particular the text at the beginning of the page. As with titles and meta-'description' statements, choosing this text carefully can influence the ranking of the pages of your journal for particular search phrases.

Keep in mind that understanding how people who would be interested in your journal, e.g. people in your scholarly field, are likely to search for content is as important as understanding how the search engines rank content. The goal is to have the journal's webpages rank highly for the search phrases *your potential readers are likely to use.* How your journal's website ranks on searches done by people who are not likely to be interested in its content is irrelevant.

Fortunately, academic disciplines tend to have their own terminology, and the search phrases used by people who would be interested in your journal are likely to be relatively unique to that particular discipline. This should be a big help in placing the journal's webpages high in the rankings of the searches done by scholars in your field, since their search phrases are likely to be relatively unique and (hopefully) consistent with the text of your journal's webpages. As will be discussed below, it is possible to find out the search terms used by people who accessed your site via a search engine. Reviewing them can be helpful in tailoring the text on your webpages to improve your journal site's search results.

Beyond tailoring the text of your webpages and including an HTML title and meta-description statement, using the strategies discussed in previous sections to get your journal on as many directories, metadata harvesters and indexes as possible can improve your search engine rankings. One of the most important criteria search engines use for determining rankings is evaluating the links from other websites to your website. The number of links is important, but links from heavily accessed sites like the Open Directory Project have a much greater impact than those from marginal sites that are not extensively linked by other sites. Most search engines rely heavily on sophisticated link analysis in determining their rankings, since it is a very good measure of the relevance of a website as well as something that is difficult to fake or manipulate by people attempting to raise the rankings of a website.

The algorithms used by search engines actually work quite well, and the most relevant and useful websites tend to end up with the highest rankings. The best strategy for getting good search engine rankings is to focus on developing a good journal with plenty of valuable content that lots of people will want to link to and access. If you do that, your journal will be ranked highly for the right reasons: because it represents a valuable resource.

Professional networking

Probably the best way of getting the word out about your journal is through the professional networks in your field. Most scholarly fields have one or more mailing lists that are commonly used by people in the field. Announcing your journal and letting colleagues know about new articles published in the journal via the mailing lists in your field can be a very effective means of dissemination, particularly when your journal is just starting up. The professional organizations in your field may be willing to send an announcement about a new OA journal to their membership mailing list. It does not cost you anything to ask. You may also be able to post notices on blogs or other types of websites that are frequented by members of the discipline. Less 'high-tech' strategies such as posting notices on physical bulletin boards at society meetings or renting space for a booth in an exhibition section are also good ways to disseminate information about a new journal.

Gathering intelligence on who is accessing your journal

Learning about the people who access the journal can be useful in making the journal more accessible. A great deal of information is available or can easily be collected on who is accessing your journal site and how they got there. Virtually all web servers keep logs that describe each request for a webpage made by someone's browser. As part of the request for a webpage, browsers also pass along information to the server that is stored in these logs along with information provided by the server itself. The exact information that is collected depends on the web server software and its configuration. Generally, logs include the IP address of the requesting browser, its URL if one is available, the referring site's URL if the request is made via a hyperlink on another site and the type of browser. Some logs also record the keywords or phrases used from the results of searches if the request is coming from a search engine.

Server logs are not easy to work with. First, they are voluminous. Since every file downloaded is logged, and most webpages include graphics and other material as separate files, a single request for a webpage can generate half a dozen or more log entries. Fortunately, there are specialized programs called log analyzers that summarize the information into user-friendly graphs, tables and lists. This log analysis can provide a wealth of useful information on who is accessing your journal's website, where they are located and how they got to your journal's site. From the IP address and URL of the browser (if provided), the analyzer software can generally tell the country and even the specific location of the computer requesting a page from the journal's site. By analyzing the whole set of logs over a period of time, the software can tell how many unique computers accessed the site over a given period, how many repeat visits there were from the same computer and how long the computer 'browsed' your site and the number of pages it accessed.

What is particularly useful is learning about the referrals to your site from hyperlinks on other sites. Knowing the number of times people were referred to your site from specific directories, search engines and indexes is very helpful in understanding the effectiveness the various strategies discussed in the preceding sections. Learning the keywords and phrases used by people who found your journal website via a search engine can also help you fine-tune the text of the webpages in your journal to increase these referrals.

As noted, there is a variety of different log analyzer software. Many are commercial but several are open source and available at no cost. Examples of open source software include Webalizer (www.webcitation.org/5Pac3GNkz) and AWStats (www.webcitation.org/5PayTJ0UC). Both are very good packages and provide a wealth of useful statistics. Unless you are operating your own server, you will probably have to use the software available on the server hosting your journal. Fortunately, most web hosting companies provide some level of log analysis, though you may have to pay extra for access to this service. If you are using an institutional server, they may have log analyzer software or you may be able to get whoever is maintaining the server to install one of the open source packages.

If you do not have access to a log analyzer, another option for tracking access to your website is through other websites that will track access on your site and provide you with statistics. To use these services you have to add snippets of code, in a programming language such JavaScript, to each webpage you would like tracked. These code snippets send information to the website that compiles it when the page with the snippet is accessed. You can then go to the site that is compiling the statistics and get the information about the pages you track. These sites provide this service to make money through advertising or to use your information for their own purposes. A very nice tracking service is provided by Google Analytics (www.webcitation.org/5Pb0N0bDz).

There is no charge for up to 5 million page views a month, and it provides incredibly detailed reports and excellent graphics describing how your journal is being accessed and by whom. As noted, you must add the code snippet to each page you would like to track, which can be tedious. If you do not have access to a log analyzer, Google Analytics or another such service can provide a valuable alternative for tracking access to your journal.

All the strategies above can help get the word out about your journal. They are particularly helpful when your journal is just starting out. Over time, dissemination of the journal will take on a life of its own. As your journal matures, you will find all sorts of sites will begin linking both to the journal and to specific articles within the journal, increasing traffic to the journal. As an OA journal, your site has a huge advantage over most websites when it comes to dissemination: it is providing valuable information at no cost. The effects can be synergistic, raising the rankings of the journal on searches, generating more traffic to your journal site, increasing the number of websites that link to your journal and further disseminating information about your journal.

Part III
Maintaining and operating an open access journal

8

Launching the journal

The preceding chapters have covered many of the salient issues in creating and operating a new OA journal. This chapter will draw on that material and discuss the process of launching a new OA journal. There are many decisions that should be made and a lot to accomplish before officially launching a new journal. Many OA journals formed by individuals or small groups of scholars fail before they ever become established. This wastes a lot of time and effort, hurts the reputation of OA journals and is a terrible disservice to the authors who entrusted the new journal with their manuscripts. Anticipating the challenges of getting a new journal established and careful planning before launching can go a long way to ensuring the journal will be successful. This chapter breaks down the process into three sections: planning for the new journal, launch preparation and launching the journal. Table 8.1 outlines the activities in each section.

The planning stage

In the planning stage a new journal should move from a vague idea to a concrete and detailed vision. During this stage you should develop both a clear conceptualization of the journal, its scope, contents and form, and a detailed plan for how it

Table 8.1 Checklist for launching a new journal

Planning for the new journal

Form editorial board and assign an editor and other key roles
Craft journal structure and attributes:

- define a scope and select a name
- choose a style guide and serial structure[a]
- define types of articles and additional sections that will be included
- create format and layout for journal pages
- define review structure and process[b]

Define journal's policies and procedures
Determine strategy for financing and obtaining necessary resources for operating journal
Decide where/how journal will be hosted, journal management software (if any) and by whom/how web development and maintenance will be managed
Develop a dissemination strategy and plan
Plan initial set of content and determine invited authors
Set tentative launch date

Launch preparation

Purchase domain name and obtain journal management and/or other necessary software; arrange for web hosting
Obtain an ISSN
Develop website, install and test journal management or other software, set up e-mail accounts and distribution lists
Develop documentation for journal policies, procedures, instructions for authors and any other documentation
Recruit invited authors for initial set of content
Recruit reviewers
Implement dissemination strategy:

- develop a 'press release' describing the journal that can be used in dissemination
- investigate the indexes, directories and search engines to which the journal will be submitted; obtain necessary information on the procedures for submitting the journal to the chosen indexes, directories and search engines
- determine listserv(s) where new articles or issues will be announced
- contact relevant professional organizations and seek their support in publicizing the journal

Table 8.1	Checklist for launching a new journal *(Cont'd)*

Prepare the content for the launch issue of the journal:

- monitor the receipt of invited articles and other content
- copy-edit and format the material for the launch issue

Upload initial content and finalize website; review and proof webpages; test submission system and all other journal software

Launching the journal

Announce journal launch and publicize journal and initial set of content through your dissemination strategy
Submit journal to directories, search engines and indexes (if appropriate)
Begin monitoring traffic to journal website

Notes
[a] Organization of the journal into volumes/issues, if manuscripts will be published as ready or by issue, how will referencing be done, e.g. page number, sequentially numbered articles etc.
[b] How the review process will be structured, reviewer selection criteria and process, timeline and flow for the review process.

will operate. You should also plan a strategy for announcing and disseminating information about the journal, and a strategy for obtaining an initial set of articles and other content with which to launch the journal. The details of the planning process are covered in Chapter 3, and it would be a good idea to go back over that chapter as you are working through the process of planning for the new journal.

A good place to start is by organizing the editorial board. Their role will be to help guide the operation of the journal, and there is no time when thoughtful advice from other experts in your scholarly field will be needed more than at this point. With the advice of your editorial board, you should begin to think about who will perform the various roles in operating the journal. Initially the effort will not be significant, but there will be tasks such as web development, layout and copy-editing that require some specialized expertise, and it will be necessary to identify someone who is willing and has the expertise to take on these roles.

Early on in the planning process, it will be necessary to define the scope of the journal and choose a title. As noted in Chapter 3, these are important for defining the journal, encouraging interest and facilitating its dissemination. Think about the types of articles and other material such as letters, editorials and/or book reviews that will be included as sections in the journal. The structure of the journal can evolve over time, but it is important to develop a clear definition of the types of material the journal will initially solicit. Determine the layout, style and the type(s) of digital format in which the contents of the journal will be published. These issues should be settled before you and your colleagues begin developing the journal's website and obtaining the necessary software for producing the final copies of the material that will be contained in the journal.

You will need to grapple with the difficult issue of how to fund and/or obtain the necessary resources for operating the journal. It is important to think through this issue and have a clear and realistic idea of how the journal will be supported and what resources are likely to be available for its operation. You may want to review Chapter 6 while addressing the journal's financing and resources. These issues will play a key role in how the journal will operate: what, if any, services will be purchased, and what tasks you and your colleagues must do yourselves or find volunteer help to accomplish.

It will be necessary to conceptualize how the submission, review, revision and manuscript preparation processes will operate, including how the review process will be structured and reviewers selected. You will also need to define the journal's policies, where the journal will be hosted and what, if any, journal management system will be used.

An important issue in launching the journal will be disseminating information about it and obtaining the initial content for the journal. This is critical. A new journal must convince authors to submit high-quality manuscripts. Given the time and effort that goes into a publishable scholarly article and the importance of publishing in high-quality peer-reviewed journals for advancement in academia, it is very difficult to convince authors to submit their work to a new journal before it develops a record of accomplishment. This will be an ongoing problem until the journal has become established and has a record of publishing high-quality articles that are widely cited. Since it is initially difficult to get authors to submit manuscripts, and in particular their best manuscripts, new journals have a real 'chicken-and-egg' problem of developing a reputation that will attract good manuscripts. Large commercial publishers can rely on their reputation, ability to attract well-known editors and the resources to mount a professional advertising campaign to launch a new journal. Without these advantages, you will have an uphill battle getting the new journal established and developing a reputation that will attract high-quality manuscripts. Use the strategies in the last chapter, and in particular your editorial board members' professional contacts, to their best advantage. Also use networking and communication avenues such as mailing lists and professional societies to let members of your field of study know about the new journal.

It is critically important to launch the journal with a set of high-quality articles and other material, ideally from well-known people in the field. This is the best way to convince authors to send you their best manuscripts. This is a time to call in every favor you and your editorial board can in getting well-respected colleagues to submit manuscripts for the launch of the journal. Have as many of the editorial board members as possible submit manuscripts as well, and include an editorial announcing the journal, its scope and the rationale behind creating it. While the manuscripts solicited for launching the journal will not be peer reviewed, make sure they are very carefully edited and only ask people you are confident will submit high-quality work. You do not want to be in the position of having to choose between publishing a manuscript that will detract from the journal or, uncomfortably, not publishing a manuscript you solicited.

Set a launch date at the point you feel you can comfortably predict when everything will be ready. At that point, you can begin the process of actively advertising the journal. As your plans for the journal gel, you and your colleagues can begin preparing for its launch. These issues are discussed in the next section.

Launch preparation

Once you have developed a clear idea of what the journal's scope, contents and form will be and a detailed plan for how it will operate, you can begin developing the materials and completing the steps necessary for launching the journal.

The step that is likely to take the most time and the one you should focus on first is obtaining the articles and other content that will make up the initial issue of the journal.[1] I suggest starting by developing a plan for what you would ideally like to have included in the initial issue and who would write these manuscripts. One option is to have the issue focus on a coherent theme. As noted above, one source of authors that you can count on to come through and produce manuscripts is your editorial board. You will want to have other authors as well, and ones as well known and influential in the field as possible. As experts in your field, you and your editorial board will certainly know some excellent candidates to approach for creating the initial issue of the journal.

Do not be afraid to ask other people whom you may not know personally. Frame it as an opportunity and an honor to be included in the first issue of a new journal, and emphasize that you are asking them given their status as a leader in the field. Aim for having at least as much initial material as would appear in a typical issue of a scholarly journal. Try to obtain commitments from substantially more authors than needed to achieve this goal. Some of the authors are likely to agree and then never complete the manuscript, and you can never have too many articles to launch the journal. Even if you have to postpone the launch waiting for some of the authors to complete their manuscripts or go back and ask additional authors for additional articles, I would urge you to do what it takes to have at least nine or ten full-length articles in the initial set of content. Other material such as book reviews, editorials and commentary can help flesh out the first issue.

It will be necessary to write the journal policies, procedures, instructions for authors and potentially other documentation such as instructions for reviewers. While the conceptualization of this material is listed in the planning stage to be consistent with the organization of this chapter, in reality you will be creating the documentation as you conceptualize the policy and procedures. This iterative process is likely to continue after the journal is launched and you revise the material based on experience. The documentation will need to be integrated into webpages and forms on the website. It will be necessary to work closely with the web developer(s) on integrating the material.

As discussed in the previous chapter, you should obtain an ISSN for the journal. This is a simple process and there is no charge. Submit the application as early as possible so that the ISSN will be available to include on any promotional material or announcements of the journal.

You will need to make a decision on how the journal will be hosted and what, if any, journal management software will be used. Make these decisions early in the development process and give yourself plenty of time to develop a website and install journal management software, particularly if you are unfamiliar with the task. As noted in Chapter 4, the Scholarly Exchange offers a means of avoiding the challenges of setting up a website and the technical issues associated with the process. There is no charge for the first year of the journal, and if you and your colleagues do not have the expertise or access to the expertise to develop a website from scratch, this can be a very attractive option.

There is a lot to develop if you are creating a new journal website, and you should give yourself several months to complete this task. It will be necessary to obtain a domain name and, depending on how your journal will be hosted, you may also need to select a web hosting company and identify someone to handle the web development tasks.

If you are hosting your own site, you may need to install the journal management system and set up e-mail account(s) and a list manager for announcing new articles. Most commercial hosting companies provide e-mail and many give access to a listserv, but it will be necessary to decide what accounts will be needed and to set them up. It will also be necessary to develop a layout for the website and possibly a logo for the journal. Someone will need to write the text for the front page and other webpages. Someone must develop a pleasing style and layout for the journal's webpages.

As noted in Chapter 4, it is *essential* to think through carefully how the website will be organized, particularly the organizational structure for the folders where manuscripts and other material that will be distributed by the journal will be stored. Once the journal begins publishing, it will be very disruptive to change its organizational structure.

Also, be very careful in designing a naming convention for the manuscript files. Use a system that is logical and makes it easy to track manuscripts. For example, you might use a prefix to indicate the section of the journal or type of article, with specific digits after the prefix indicating the year or volume, issue (if any) and sequential number for the manuscript. Keep in mind that, however the system is designed, it will be terribly disruptive to change it at a later point in time. Since readers, indexes and in some cases directories will create hyperlinks directly to the manuscripts in the journal, the URL, which reflects the directory structure and specific name of the manuscript file, should never change.

The website and associated software should be carefully reviewed and tested. Any written material should be carefully edited and checked for typographical or spelling errors. The submission/review software, if used, should be thoroughly tested and the journal's e-mail account(s) should be checked to be sure they are working. Back-up and archival procedures and software should also be piloted.

Once you have a firm launch date, you can begin getting ready to publicize the journal. Develop a written announcement of your journal that you can use to disseminate information about it through a variety of sources. The announcement should be short, concise and focus on the scope, content and audience for the journal. Encourage readers to submit articles and, if appropriate, solicit potential reviewers. Provide links to the homepage, instructions for authors and, if appropriate, the page for volunteering to be a reviewer. Be sure to include whom to contact for more information.

Research and determine the indexes, directories and search engines to which you will submit the journal. Contact professional organizations in your field and ask if it would be possible to announce the journal through their mailing lists, newsletters or other means of communicating with their members. Identify other mailing lists, blogs or other informal communication mechanisms that can be used to disseminate information about the journal to people in your field. If you and/or your editorial board members are attending conferences in the near future, consider submitting a poster or obtaining a booth, or just take plenty of flyers of the announcement of the journal with you to distribute at the conference and post on bulletin boards. While you should develop the announcement and prepare for disseminating the journal well before the launch date, it will be best to wait until the website is ready and the material available before making a real effort to disseminate information about the journal to its potential readers. Having people access a website under construction without content is not going to be very effective and can actually be detrimental.

It will be necessary to design a workflow and process for the review, revision and preparation for publication of the submitted manuscripts. Depending on the format(s) in which you decide to publish articles and other material, it may be necessary to obtain and learn to use desktop publishing software or identify people with the necessary skills to prepare manuscripts for publication. Preparing the manuscripts that have been solicited for the initial content of the journal can serve to pilot the process as well as the systems used to monitor submissions through review, revision and publication.

Launching the journal

Once all the initial content has been uploaded and the website and all associated software carefully edited and tested, the journal can be officially launched. Now is the time to put your full energy into publicizing the journal.

Send out the prepared announcement to the mailing lists, blogs and any other outlets you were able to identify for publicizing the journal.

Now that the journal website contains the initial set of content, you can submit the site to the directories and search engines you identified in your plan for dissemination. You and your editorial board should use all your informal professional contacts to disseminate information about the launch of the journal. Both you and the editorial board should also use every opportunity at professional meetings to highlight the journal. This is an excellent way to inform the relevant people about the journal.

Begin monitoring log analysis and/or any tracking sites with which you have registered the journal's webpages to assess both the volume of traffic and where it is coming from. This will give you a good idea of how well your dissemination plan is working and what seems to be effective. The information can then be used to target your efforts in the future.

Getting a new OA journal established takes time and persistence. Be patient, but also be relentless in promoting the journal using every avenue at your disposal. It is very important to encourage submissions. Use your and your editorial board's professional contacts to solicit manuscript submissions. Since authors will still be somewhat reluctant to submit their best work, you will need to tread a fine line between publishing poor-quality manuscripts and having so little new content that the journal is not taken seriously.

There is no reason why you cannot continue to solicit articles to supplement the articles that are submitted while the journal is getting off the ground. It you are able to solicit high-quality articles in addition to the ones you are receiving as submissions, this will speed up the process of getting the journal established.

There is no easy answer to addressing the challenge of getting a new OA journal established. It will take some time, which is not all bad. It will give you and your colleagues a chance to develop and refine the process of operating the journal and managing the submission, review and manuscript preparation processes.

Continue to use the tools discussed in Chapter 7. These will help disseminate information about the journal to a wide audience. Your personal effort, contacts and knowledge of your field's informal and formal communication mechanisms are likely to be the most effective means of gaining readership and submissions that will cement the new journal's reputation as a high-quality, established journal to which scholars will want to submit their best manuscripts. Many new OA journals have accomplished this. So can yours.

Note

1. I am using 'issue' in a general sense here for the content with which the journal will be launched, even though you may not be organizing and publishing the journal as issues.

9

Maintaining and sustaining an OA journal

Once your new journal has been launched, you will need to focus on the open-ended tasks of maintaining and sustaining it. It is likely to take some time before the journal will begin receiving a significant number of manuscript submissions. This lull is likely to last a year or two, but can go on longer. How quickly the journal becomes established will be influenced by many factors, including the quality of the material in the initial issue, how well you are able to publicize the journal and how comfortable people in your field are with publishing in an electronic-only OA journal. Although waiting for submissions to pick up may be frustrating, it will give you and your colleagues a chance to become proficient in managing the review and publication processes.

Table 9.1 outlines the steps in the review, publication and journal maintenance processes. You can choose to organize these processes in different ways, but for the most part you will need to address each of the steps.

Managing the review process

Tracking the process

Depending how you designed the journal, manuscripts will be submitted either through a web-based submission form

Table 9.1   Review, publication and journal maintenance processes

Peer-review process Receipt of submission Determine if appropriate for review Preparation for review Selection of reviewers Contact reviewers/provide material Monitor review process Organize review material and reread manuscript Make decision and provide feedback to authors Manage revision process (if necessary)
Processing other types of material Book reviews Letters to the editor Commentary
Manuscript preparation process Copy-editing Formatting and typesetting Formatting and preparing figures and tables Preparing metadata and, optionally, an archival version in XML
Publication process Integration into website Notifying readers
Maintenance processes Maintaining reviewer pool Record-keeping and handling requests for information Documentation

or via e-mail. The first step of the process is to enter information concerning the submission into a tracking system. If you are using a journal management system, this will be taken care of automatically. In either case, you will need some way to track the manuscript through the review and publication processes. A new submission record should be started at the point a manuscript is received. If you are tracking the manuscripts manually, at minimum you should assign some type of identifier as an efficient means of labeling each submission and record the date submitted, title and author contact information. The system, whether electronic or manual, should track each submission through the review process to its final disposition. Questions will come up as to the status of manuscripts for a variety of reasons, even if the manuscript is rejected without being reviewed. Keeping good records will save you a lot of trouble in the long run. Tracking will also help ensure manuscripts do not get lost in the system and languish until an irate author contacts you wanting to know what has happened to their submission.

Preliminary review

The next step in the process is to do a preliminary review of the manuscript to determine if it fits within the scope of the journal and meets any other requirements outlined in the instructions for authors. It is also a good idea to assess whether the manuscript is of high enough quality to be sent out for peer review. Since the editor will be making the final publication decision, if in your view the manuscript is clearly not publishable, it is pointless to send it out for external review.[1] It is in the best interest of both the journal and the author to notify authors immediately that their manuscripts have been rejected and give the reason why you feel they are not publishable.

As part of the initial review, check the submission to see if the authors have followed the submission guidelines and the manuscript is appropriately formatted. You may wish to allow authors to submit manuscripts that are not correctly formatted, with the understanding that, if accepted, the authors will revise the manuscript to meet the journal's formatting criteria. Since manuscripts are often submitted sequentially to more than one journal before being accepted, as long as the manuscript is in a reasonable format for review it makes little sense to require an author to spend time reformatting the manuscript to fit the journal's specific requirements until it is clear it will be accepted. However, if the manuscript is not in the journal's required format, be sure to make it clear to the corresponding author that if the manuscript is accepted, it will need to be formatted correctly at that point. This will avoid any misunderstanding. Also be sure to check that authors have followed any requirements in the author agreement, such as guidelines for research on human subjects or indicating any potential conflicts.

Preparing manuscripts for review

The next step, if the manuscript has not been rejected in the initial review by the editor, is to prepare the manuscript for review. Many journals remove any identifying information so the reviewers do not know the identity of the authors or their institution. The choice of whether or not to blind the review copy of manuscripts is of course up to you and your colleagues. If you decide to do so, you may want to ask the authors in the instructions to create and submit a blinded copy and save you the effort. In addition, it is helpful for the reviewers to have the review copy double-spaced. Be sure to include page numbers so the reviewers can reference these in their feedback. You many also want to turn on the line-numbering feature available in most word processing programs to help the reviewers identify specific locations in the manuscript when providing feedback. Add a statement in the header of each page clearly stating the name of the journal, that this is a review copy of the manuscript and that it is copyrighted material owned by the authors and not for distribution.

Selecting reviewers

The number of reviewers used for each review is up to you. I would strongly recommend attempting to have at least three or four per manuscript. Good reviewers provide a wealth of feedback, but all reviewers have blind spots and a specific point of view. While some of the feedback will be redundant, each reviewer will provide a unique perspective and some different ideas about the strengths and weaknesses of the manuscript. Having several reviewers will provide a much better basis for both deciding if the manuscript should be published and giving the author constructive feedback even if the work is not published by the journal.

Ask several more reviewers than the minimum you feel are needed to review the manuscript. Not all will agree, and some who agree may not return the review. Even if it turns out that all the reviewers agree and return their reviews, it never hurts to have extra feedback.

Be sure to specify in the request to review a date by which the review should be returned and any other instructions. At *MEO* we give reviewers four weeks to complete the review. I feel this is more than adequate, and giving reviewers additional time just results in them putting off doing the review until it is closer to the final date.

As the reviewers agree to review, they will need to be sent a copy of the manuscript and a review form. The whole process of asking reviewers to participate in a review and sending out materials can be automated via a web-based review system; if not, it will have to be via manually sending out e-mails, which can be time-consuming. If you are soliciting reviewers via e-mail, be sure to keep good records of the reviewers who have been asked and which have agreed to review. This information will be needed for a variety of purposes beyond managing the specific review. It will be necessary to keep track of who has recently reviewed manuscripts so that you do not overload specific reviewers. It is also common for reviewers to ask for documentation of how many manuscripts they have reviewed to aid in their own annual assessments and promotion and tenure reviews.

Managing the review

Microsoft Word format seems to be the universal format for written documents, and is the one you should use for distributing manuscripts and review forms. Keeping the review copy of the manuscript in a word processing format will allow reviewers to add comments and suggestions for edits directly in the manuscript. In my experience many reviewers like to do this, and it can be very helpful to the authors in revising their manuscripts.

Be sure to track the reviewers who agree to review and the date they agreed. After a reasonable period waiting to receive agreement (I usually allow about a week), if there are still not enough reviewers, ask some additional reviewers from the journal's reviewer pool.

Use some type of calendaring system, if it is not built into your journal management system, to remind you when the reviews are due for each manuscript under review. Otherwise, the due dates for reviews can easily be missed. A week or so before the reviews are due, send out a reminder to any reviewers who have not returned their reviews. Obviously you should be polite and indicate they still have a week to complete the review, noting that you are just ensuring it did not slip their minds.

If you are not using a journal management system and are communicating with the reviewers via e-mail, it is helpful to have all the standard correspondence for the review process, such as requests to review and reminders, developed as templates that you can just copy and add names/dates etc. This will save you a tremendous amount of time and effort as compared with writing every e-mail individually.

When the reviews are due, there are likely to be some that have not been received. At this point you can send out a second reminder and give reviewers another week or so. Unless you have not received an adequate number of reviews, I suggest stopping at that point and using the reviews that are available to make a decision and develop feedback to the author. It is unfair to keep authors waiting for weeks because a reviewer is not responsible enough to return a review. If you feel you need additional reviews, ask one of the editorial board members or a colleague you know well and trust to review the manuscript as quickly as possible.

The review decision and feedback letter

At this point you will need to make a publication decision and provide feedback to the authors. Reread the manuscript carefully to familiarize yourself with it again and develop your sense of its strengths and weaknesses. I find it helpful to make notes directly in the manuscript as I read it. After reading the manuscript, review the feedback from the reviewers. They will probably identify issues that you missed, and may have a somewhat different point of view as to the strengths and weaknesses of the manuscript. After reading and considering their feedback, make the publication decision. It generally makes sense to use three categories: accept as is, accept with revisions, or reject.

Deciding whether to accept with extensive revisions or reject a manuscript can be difficult. Feedback from reviewers is helpful, but in my experience the feedback from multiple reviewers is often inconsistent, with some feeling a 'borderline' manuscript should be rejected and others feeling it should be revised. In the end it is the editor's decision. Some manuscripts are clearly too flawed to be published, but most reside somewhere between perfect and awful. This is a subjective decision, and you just need to use your own judgment. The feedback from the reviewers can be helpful, but it is just that, feedback, and it is your decision as editor that is final.

It is rare to receive manuscripts that are so well written that they cannot benefit from revisions. If a manuscript is very well written and clearly worthy of publication, you may provide some feedback but let the author make the decision as to what, if any, revisions are needed.

It is helpful to send the authors all the feedback from the reviewers, with the exception of comments the reviewer clearly designated as for the editor only. For manuscripts that are accepted with revisions, be very clear in stating exactly what revisions are necessary and that the author is not obligated to incorporate every suggestion from each reviewer. The feedback from multiple reviewers is often vague and occasionally contradictory, and if there are more than a couple of reviewers the feedback can get voluminous. Be very specific about what you feel are the key issues that need to be addressed in the revision, and then you can suggest that the authors review the full set of feedback and use their own judgment in deciding what additional suggestions to implement.

When manuscripts are accepted with revisions, ask the authors to confirm whether or not they are willing to complete the revisions. Also either give the authors a due date for their revised manuscript or ask them to commit to a date by which they will complete the revisions. Asking authors to finalize the manuscript by a specific date helps ensure that they complete the revisions. Without a specific deadline, it is not uncommon for an author to put the task aside and never get around to completing the revisions. It is also a good idea to put a reminder in your calendar to contact the author if the revisions are not finished by the due date. Given the tremendous amount of work that goes into creating a publishable journal article and the key role publishing in peer-reviewed journals plays in promotion and tenure decisions, it always amazes me how frequently authors need to be prodded to complete what are sometimes minor revisions in order to complete the publication process and get credit for a peer-reviewed article.

When you send the feedback on a manuscript to the authors, send a copy to each reviewer who completed the review. This is a simple thing to do, and reviewers really appreciate receiving a copy of the feedback sent to the author. They like to know the final disposition of the manuscript, and are particularly interested in how the other reviewers rated the manuscript and what feedback they provided.

When the author returns the revised manuscript, be sure to check that it has been revised to your satisfaction and has addressed each of the points noted in your feedback letter. Also check to be sure that the manuscript is formatted correctly, and remember to update the status of the manuscript in your records.

Publishing other types of material

You may wish to publish other types of material, such as book reviews, letters to the editor, editorials and/or commentary. Such material is generally not peer reviewed but still requires editorial review. With the exception of peer review, these types of material are processed in much the same way as peer-reviewed articles. You will need to develop a submission process and procedures for reviewing these types of manuscripts. If you are creating metadata for indexing and archiving your articles, you will most likely want to do the same for these materials.

You should state in your instructions for authors what additional types of material the journal publishes, the requirements for the various types of manuscripts and how they should be formatted and submitted. It may be helpful to review the instructions for authors in a variety of scholarly journals to get ideas on what material other than peer-reviewed articles you will accept for publication and how it should be formatted and processed.

Book reviews

Book reviews are somewhat different to other types of material that you may publish. If you decide to include book reviews in your journal, they are generally received in three ways. Publishers or authors may ask to have a book reviewed; scholars may submit unsolicited reviews; or you and your editorial board may choose on your own to review a particular book or solicit someone to review the book.

Publishers and authors view book reviews as a very effective and inexpensive way to advertise new books. Once you add a book review section to your journal and let it be known that you will be publishing book reviews, you will probably start being contacted by publishers with requests to review books. If you accept the request, the publisher or author will generally send you a complimentary copy of the book and it will be up to you to identify someone to do the review. In addition, you may have authors submit unsolicited book reviews, although in my experience this is far less common than being contacted by a publisher or an author. It is also possible that there will be such a seminal book published in your field that you and your editorial board might decide on your own to review the book.

The biggest challenge in publishing book reviews is getting reviewers to complete the review. Unlike article reviews, there is only a single reviewer and the review of a book is a much bigger task than the review of an article. *MEO* still occasionally publishes book reviews, but several years ago I began declining requests from publishers because of this issue. I found it relatively easy to find someone willing to review a book, either asking a colleague with an interest in the topic or an experienced reviewer from our peer-review pool – but quite often they never completed the review, despite repeated reminders. I believe publishers are cognizant of this problem and their investment is small, but it still is embarrassing to accept a copy of a new book and never publish a review. If you decide to publish book reviews and accept requests from publishers and authors, be very careful about whom you ask to review them. It is a bigger task than most people realize and, at least in my experience, many people fail to complete the review. Junior faculty, who are often very eager to enhance their publication record, are a good choice. They are enthusiastic, interested in taking on the task, and in my experience more likely to compete the review. They may require more mentoring in the review and revision process; however, you are not only providing a service to your field and the author and publisher, but also helping in advancing the career of the faculty member.

Letters to the editor

Letters to the editor is another common section in scholarly journals. It generally contains commentary the author wishes to voice, or in some cases research or other scholarship that does not reach the level of quality of a peer-reviewed article.

If you decide to accept letters to the editor, you will receive some as unsolicited submissions. You may also offer some of the authors who have manuscripts rejected the opportunity to publish their material as letters to the editor. This is a reasonable option for manuscripts that do not meet what you feel are your minimum standards for a peer-reviewed article but still have some merit and would be of interest to readers.

Editorials and commentary

You or your colleagues involved in publishing the journal may wish to write occasional editorials on topics pertinent to your field or the operation of the journal. You may also invite others to provide commentary or accept unsolicited manuscripts. You may or may not choose to peer review these submissions. Some journals editors choose to write short editorials with each issue, particularly if issues are based around a theme. The *JEP* is one example of such a journal, and this practice is also occasionally used by *IR*.

Manuscript preparation process

Copy-editing

The first step in the preparing a manuscript for publication after the author has completed any revisions is copy-editing. Copy-editing is time-consuming and takes someone who is a skilled editor. The copy-editor should also be familiar with the technical language and style of the particular field of study. It is usually difficult to find someone who has these skills and is willing to volunteer the significant time necessary to do a good job of copy-editing. I have found copy-editing to be one of the most difficult challenges of operating a small OA journal based largely on volunteer effort.

One option is to put the burden on the authors, making it an expectation that they will provide the final version of their manuscripts in a form suitable for publication. BioMed Central, a commercial publisher of around 200 OA biomedical journals, uses this approach for many of its journals and it seems to work reasonably well. Based on my experience with *MEO*, I have not found placing the burden of copy-editing solely on the author a satisfactory approach. Many authors do submit final copies of their manuscripts that are well written and largely free of typographical, grammatical and spelling errors. Other manuscripts need a great deal of editing to be publishable. Electronic journals by nature are international, and a significant number of the manuscripts your journal is likely to receive will be from authors whose primary language is not the language in which the journal is published. These manuscripts generally need substantial editing, and it can be extremely time-consuming. Asking these authors to find someone who can edit their manuscripts is often not practical.

One option if you have adequate funding is to use a copy-editing service. There are many of these services, and they can easily be found by doing a search on the web. They generally provide different levels of editing, and may charge more when the author is not a native speaker of the language. One issue with these services is that, as noted above, ideally the copy-editor should be familiar with the terminology and style of writing typically used in your field of study. They can, however, save you a great deal of time by addressing many of the language problems in the manuscript, reducing the work required by you and your colleagues. One advantage of contracting for copy-editing on a per-article basis is that you can try different copy-editing services until you find one that works well for you, without any additional cost or inconvenience. This will also allow you to contract only for copy-editing for those manuscripts that need additional editing. One option we have considered at *MEO* but have not implemented is asking authors whose manuscripts are in need of significant copy-editing to pay the cost of getting their manuscript professionally edited. The manuscripts we receive that need extensive copy-editing are generally authored by people for whom English is a second language. These authors are often from developing countries, and are unlikely to have the resources to pay the costs of a copy-editing service. I have found no simple solution to this problem.

Formatting for publication

After the articles are copy-edited, they will need to be formatted for publication. How this is done will be determined in part by the format(s) in which manuscripts will be published. As noted earlier, the majority of journals publish in either PDF or HTML, or both. One of the many advantages of PDF is that there is software that can directly convert the print files from virtually any software program directly into PDF format.

If you choose to publish your manuscripts in PDF, you can format them in a word processor such as Microsoft Word and convert them directly into PDF for distribution. Adobe was the developer of the format, and the most common software for creating PDFs is Adobe Acrobat, but there is other software that can create PDF files. For example, Open Office Writer, an open source package very similar to Microsoft Word, can generate PDF files directly. As discussed earlier, if you provide a template and insist that authors use this for creating the final copy of their manuscript submitted for publication, you can significantly reduce the effort required to format and produce good-quality manuscripts for publication.

With a full-featured word processor such as Microsoft Word or Open Office Writer, you can produce documents that are close to typeset in quality. This, however, takes additional effort, and it can sometimes be very difficult to lay out documents with a large number of tables and figures. Another option is to use desktop publishing software specifically designed to create the layout for published documents. There will be an additional cost in purchasing the software if you do not already have access to it, and there is a significant learning curve involved in mastering the software. However, desktop publishing software such as Adobe's Indesign can produce significantly higher-quality documents, on par with professionally published journal articles. Once the software has been mastered, it is also much easier to create the layout for a complex article with a number of tables and figures. Whether it is worth the cost and effort to purchase and master desktop publishing software in order to generate higher-quality published articles is up to you. It is certainly possible to publish a professional-looking journal without it.

As noted in Chapter 3, the majority of readers prefer PDF, and in fact a number of OA journals, including the *JMIR*, provide HTML-formatted articles for free but charge for the PDF versions as a means of generating income. PDF does have some disadvantages. Since it is not possible to embed programming scripts in PDF files, as it is in HTML files, you have less flexibility in tracking access and creating dynamic content than with HTML files. Servers do log access to PDF files, but services such as Google Analytics will not be able to track PDFs. If you choose to generate income to operate the journal via advertising, it is not possible to include advertising on PDF files as it is with HTML files. Since other sites and individuals will often link directly to the PDF articles rather than other pages on your website, this could significantly reduce the amount of income that is generated by advertising. Despite these disadvantages, PDF is an excellent choice for disseminating the material in your journal and generally preferred by readers.

HTML is also a good choice for distributing the material in your journal. Although it is becoming less and less of a problem, HTML documents are generally smaller and more universally accessible, particularly for people in developing countries. HTML also has some disadvantages. It is not possible to achieve typeset-quality documents, as with PDFs, and HTML does not really support pagination – which is a significant disadvantage. Also, if you receive manuscripts in a word processing format, it will require some effort to convert manuscripts into HTML format.

If you choose to distribute your manuscripts in HTML, you should develop a template that can be used to format the manuscripts efficiently. You can then make the template available to authors, and at least request they use it for formatting the final version of their manuscripts into HTML. While not every author may have the expertise and capability to convert manuscripts into HTML, it may avoid some of the work you and/or your colleagues will have to do formatting manuscripts. *IR* uses this approach for its manuscript submissions, and its template provides a good example of how to design a template (www.webcitation.org/ 5Q9juGEVZ). The instructions for authors in *IR* caution authors not to use Microsoft Word or FrontPage to convert to or develop their documents in HTML, and I agree. While the HTML documents produced by these programs look fine in Internet Explorer, in my experience they do not always display appropriately in other browsers and the HTML code they generate is voluminous and can be very difficult to work with in HTML editors.

It is also a good idea to use cascading style sheets (CSS) for defining the style elements of the template. CSS are becoming widely used in web development and have a number of advantages over including style elements directly in the HTML code. They allow the developer to define the style elements separately from the text of webpages, and can be contained either within the webpage or in a separate file. Storing the CSS style information for articles in a separate set of files that are accessed by all the articles will allow you to change the look of your articles by changing the CSS in one file rather than in each article. CSS are becoming the preferred approach to styling HTML, and you should use these throughout your site.

Preparing figures and tables

Preparing figures and tables for publication can be challenging. As noted in Chapter 5, it is a good idea to specify in the instructions for authors how you would like tables and figures represented in the submission. Most journals ask authors to note the location in the manuscript where the table/figure will be placed, and attach the actual table/figure at the end of the document. This simplifies the formatting process.

It is also a good idea to specify that authors use the table creation feature in their word processor for creating tables. Microsoft Word and other common word processing programs such as Open Office Writer have a table creation feature. Using this feature will standardize how tables are represented, facilitate formatting the document for publication and ensure the consistency of how tables are presented. You may also want to specify how tables should look, and provide a template authors can use for at least simple tables.

Figures can also be a problem when creating the formatted version of a manuscript. Many journals require authors to provide figures as publication-ready graphics files in a standard format. This simplifies the process of producing the published version of an article and ensures that published figures are of high quality.

It has been my experience, however, that authors often use graphics tools within Microsoft Word or word processors to produce the figures in their manuscripts. If you are using Microsoft Word or Open Office Writer to create the published version of the manuscript in PDF, this is not a problem since the figure can remain within the document and has the same resolution as when created. However, if you are producing HTML versions of the manuscript for publication or are transferring the document to a desktop publishing system such as Adobe Indesign, you will need to extract or convert the graphic image into a standard graphics format. I have had difficulty retrieving figures created with the graphics tools within Microsoft Word as graphics files of a quality suitable for publication. The most effective solution I have found to date is to use the following procedure.

- Isolate the figures as a separate Word document.
- Create a PDF version of the Word document.
- From within Adobe Acrobat, save the document in a standard graphics format. (Acrobat offers a number of graphics formats as options when saving a document.)
- Use a graphics package to crop and size the figure.

Although there is a slight reduction in the quality of the image, I have found the images created using the steps above to be reasonably sharp and clear even when they contain text with a small point size. It should work for virtually any figure or other image that is embedded in a word processing document where the author is not able to provide a 'camera-ready' graphics image.

If you do not have Adobe Acrobat but do have a graphics package that can capture your computer screen as an image, it is possible to display the figure on the screen and capture it that way, and then crop it in the graphics package. I have used this approach as well, but it does not produce as sharp an image as using Acrobat.

While most journals publish in either PDF or HTML, many also create extendable markup language (XML) versions of their material for archival purposes. XML has a number of advantages for long-term archiving of documents. It is also required if you wish to store your manuscripts in some archives, for example PubMed Central. It is, however, difficult and extremely time-consuming to code manuscripts into XML by hand. There are commercial software packages that will convert standard word processing files into XML, but they are extremely expensive. The Public Knowledge Project is working on an open source system that will convert documents in Word or Open Office formats into XML. Current information about the project can be found at http://pkp.sfu.ca/lemon8.

Publication process

Journal organization

Traditionally, scholarly journals have been organized into volumes and issues, where issues are the basic journal publishing unit. This is necessary with print journals since, for practical reasons, the articles within the journal need to be bound into manageable units for distribution. Again for convenience, issues are published at regular intervals. With the development of electronic distribution, it became practical to publish and distribute articles individually at the point they are ready for publication. Many electronic journals continue to organize articles into monthly or quarterly issues. The choice is up to you, but I see little value in holding back articles ready for publication so that they can be distributed grouped into issues. The only exception would be when the articles are grouped in a compendium around a theme.

If you decide to publish articles as they are ready, it will be necessary to let interested readers know that new material has been added to the journal. Electronic mailing lists work very well for this process. Be sure to include the title, author(s), abstract and a hyperlink to the full manuscript in your notice. Most web hosting companies provide some type of mailing list software that you can set up to give interested readers the ability to sign up to receive notices of new material in the journal. Be sure to put directions for signing up, and also for removing one's e-mail address from the list, in a prominent place in the journal. Also include these instructions in each notice sent out through the mailing list.

It is a good idea to send out notices of new material on the major mailing list(s) in your field. This will increase dissemination and provide a constant reminder to people in the field of the journal's existence. Even if you decide to organize your material into regularly published issues, announcing them on the major mailing lists in your field, along with some 'highlights' promoting articles of interest, is a good way to publicize the journal.

It will be necessary, of course, for the person maintaining the journal website to upload new material, integrate it into the journal and update the metadata. If you add metadata at the article level to sites such as the DOAJ, this will need to be updated as well.

Journal maintenance processes

Journals, like any complex system, need some ongoing review and maintenance. It is a good idea for the editorial board to step back and do a comprehensive review of the journal and its scope and practices at periodic intervals. Some issues that should be considered include:

- the scope of the journal and how it might be revised
- the journal's operating procedures and documentation
- types of manuscripts and other material published, potential new formats, revision of existing formats and possibly dropping types of material
- updating the look and feel of the journal website and its organization, layout and format
- the journal's sources of funding and support.

These are the types of issues that can be considered at a retreat or annual editorial board meeting. They do not necessarily have to be reviewed frequently or all at once, but it is a good idea to step back and take a careful look at the journal every so often.

Managing the reviewer pool

Maintaining a viable pool of external reviewers takes some effort. People change careers, lose interest, retire or pass away, and over time there is a natural turnover of reviewers. In addition, some external reviewers do a much better job than others, and there are some who are not particularly helpful, if not detrimental. You will continually need to add people to your reviewer pool and remove those who are no longer able to continue or interested in reviewing. You should also monitor the review activity, responsiveness to requests to review and the quality and timeliness of your reviewers, so that poor reviewers can be removed from the pool.

There are a variety of ways in which you can solicit reviewers. At *MEO* we have found it valuable simply to ask for volunteers on the journal website, allowing interested people to apply by completing a web form with the necessary information. In addition, when our pool of available reviewers starts getting low, we put out an announcement requesting people to sign up to review on one of the major mailing lists in the field. We only have to do this every few years, and usually about 50 or 60 potential reviewers sign up on DR-ED, the major mailing list in medical education.

When people volunteer to review via our reviewer sign-up form, their qualifications are then reviewed and individuals who appear competent are added to the reviewer pool. We are not terribly selective, because over time we have found that the types of qualifications given in a curriculum vitae do not always predict the quality of reviewers. Instead we give anyone who appears to have a legitimate interest and some experience in medical education a chance to review, and then see how they perform. We always include several reviewers who we know do a good job, and then add some new reviewers when sending out requests to review a manuscript. That way we can be assured of having a reasonable amount of good feedback while seeing how new reviewers perform.

You should keep good records on your reviewers and periodically go through those records, dropping reviewers who rarely agree to review, are constantly tardy or do not return reviews and/or do not provide thoughtful, constructive feedback. It is essential to keep good records for this purpose. You should track when a reviewer is asked to review, whether they accept, whether they return the review, the date the review was due and the date it was completed. At *MEO* we have built into our journal management system the ability easily to add comments on the quality of a reviewer's feedback during the review process. This way, when evaluating our reviewers, we have our review editors' assessment of the quality of a reviewer's feedback along with the more objective information about their willingness to review and how timely they are in returning reviews. Our journal management system is also designed to generate a reviewer report giving a summary of their review history, comments by our review editors and the ability to access their actual reviews. This way our managing editors can systematically review the performance of our reviewers on a regular basis, dropping reviewers who are not doing a good job or rarely agreeing to review.

Record-keeping and requests for information

You will from time to time receive requests for information concerning the journal and its operation. Reviewers will often ask for verification of their review history for promotion/tenure assessment or annual evaluations. Authors will request information about the status of submissions, or occasionally about their published or rejected manuscripts. You will also occasionally receive requests by authors to verify that they have published a manuscript and that the journal is peer reviewed. Sometimes there will be requests for information about the journal itself. Keeping adequate records is essential, and will allow you to address most types of questions quickly and easily. Once again, journal management software can take care of most of your record-keeping tasks with little or no effort on your part.

Documentation

Documentation is something that is easy to forget once your journal has become established. But operating procedures change, and you may update the content in the journal, purchase new software or host your journal on a different server. Be sure to keep the journal's documentation up to date. Also be sure there are multiple people with some familiarity with the various roles and activities required to maintain the journal. Unfortunately people get sick or incapacitated, or occasionally pass away unexpectedly. The key knowledge for operating your journal should not, if at all possible, rest in one person's mind. Hopefully it will never be needed, but to ensure the continued operation of the journal ensure there is adequate documentation of the procedures required to operate the journal and that someone else at least has a basic grasp of all the key activities required to run the journal.

Note

1. This section is written as though the reader is the editor.

10

Concluding remarks

One of the major hurdles in starting a new journal without the support of a publisher is the specialized knowledge and skills required to create and operate a peer-reviewed journal. The expertise necessary to operate a journal cuts across a variety of disciplines in which most faculty have little knowledge or experience. Addressing this issue has been the central focus of this book, with the goal of facilitating the development of OA journal projects by small groups of scientists and other scholars who have little or no experience in operating a journal.

The final chapter of this book was originally intended to be an annotated bibliography of resources for the development and maintenance of small OA journal projects, many of which have already been mentioned throughout the book. It dawned on me that such a bibliography would quickly become outdated and lose its usefulness. Instead of including a static bibliography or resource guide in print, it is being published as part of the book's website (www.developing-oa-journals.org). This will allow the resource guide to be continually updated and make it available to anyone who is interested in accessing it, even if they have not purchased the book. There is also a mechanism for readers to submit suggestions for additional content and notify me of items needing updates.

One of my concerns about writing this book is that it reflects my personal views and biases on creating OA journals. I have tried to counter this by providing examples of other successful OA journals. The website also contains a bulletin board, with the hope of promoting an interactive discussion that will allow further input from others on the issues involved in creating OA journals. Along with hopefully providing a variety of views and opinions on creating and operating OA journals, it is intended serve as a means of addressing questions on creating these journals.

Please access the website and use the interactive tools to give your thoughts or questions on developing OA journals. I welcome constructive feedback on the book: what it is lacking, differences of opinion, and any outright errors in what is written. At some point I hope to produce a second edition of the book which can incorporate the feedback that has been provided. I encourage you to access the website and make use of the resources, as well as giving feedback on how both the book and the website could be improved.

References

Where feasible, reference URLs have been archived in Webcite and the Webcite URL is given in the reference. Webcite provides a permanent record of the referenced webpage that includes the original URL.

Association of Research Libraries (2004) *Monograph and Serial Expenditures*; available at: *www.webcitation.org/ 5LramQyB8* (accessed: 13 January 2007).

Baxt, W.G., Waeckerle, J.F., Berlin, J. and Callahm, M.L. (1998) 'Who reviews the reviewers? Feasibility of using fictitious manuscripts to evaluate peer reviewer performance', *Annals of Emergency Medicine*, 32: 310–17.

Bergstrom, C.T. (2002) *The Economics of Journal Publishing*; available at: *www.webcitation.org/5Lrapz5I9* (accessed: 13 January 2007).

Brown, S. (2007) '*Nature* ends experiment with open peer review, as responses are disappointing', *Chronicle of Higher Education*, 11 January; available at: *http://chronicle.com/ daily/2007/01/2007011102n.htm* (accessed: 17 October 2007).

Chicago Manual of Style (2007) *Chicago Manual of Style Online*; available at: *www.webcitation.org/5OGdYwPBH* (accessed: 21 April 2007).

Coffin, J. (2006) 'Analysis of open source principles in diverse collaborative communities', *First Monday*, 11(6); available at: *www.webcitation.org/5LrbeGIM9* (accessed: 13 January 2007).

Crow, R. (2006) 'Publishing cooperatives: an alternative for non-profit publishers', *First Monday*, 11(9); available at: *www.webcitation.org/5M2HBRqqz* (accessed: 20 January 2007).

Gøtzsche, P.C. (1989) 'Methodology and overt and hidden bias in reports of 196 double-blinded trials of non-steroidal anti-inflammatory drugs in rheumatoid arthritis', *Controlled Clinical Trials*, 10: 31–56.

Guédon, J. (2001) 'In Oldenburg's long shadow: librarians, research scientists, publishers, and the control of scientific publishing', paper presented at May meeting of Association of Research Libraries; available at: *www. webcitation.org/5LraxWswk* (accessed: 13 January 2007).

Harnad, S. (2003) 'Open access to peer-reviewed research through author/institution self-archiving: maximizing research impact by maximizing online access', *Journal of Postgraduate Medicine*, 49(4): 337–42; available at: *www. webcitation.org/5Lrb1iFYD* (accessed: 13 January 2007).

ICMJE (2007) *Uniform Requirements for Manuscripts Submitted to Biomedical Journals*; available at: *www. webcitation.org/5OAZfA0Yk* (accessed: 17 April 2007).

ISSN International Centre (2007) 'What is an ISSN?'; available at: *www.webcitation.org/5Pghuxy0h* (accessed: 18 June 2007).

Jefferson. T. (2006) 'Quality and value: models of quality control for scientific research', *Nature*; available at: *www. webcitation.org/5MZhMcDUs* (accessed: 11 February 2007).

Kaufman-Will Group (2005) *The Facts About Open Access*; available at: *www.alpsp.org/ngen_public/article.asp?id= 200&did=47&aid=270&st=&oaid=-1* (accessed: 7 August 2007).

Kronick, D.A. (1976) *A History of Scientific and Technical Periodicals: The Origins and Development of the Scientific and Technical Press 1665–1790*. Metuchen, NJ: Scarecrow Press.

Kumashiro, K.K. (2005) 'Thinking collaboratively about the peer-review process for journal-article publication', *Harvard Educational Review*, 75(3): 257–87.

Meadows, A.J. (1980) *Development of Science Publishing in Europe*. Amsterdam: Elsevier Science Publishers.

OpCit Project (2006) 'The effect of open access and downloads ("hits") on citation impact: a bibliography of studies'; available at: *www.webcitation.org/5LrbGytZr* (accessed: 13 January 2007).

Parang, E. and Saunders, L. (1994) 'SPEC Kit 202 electronic journals in ARL libraries: issues and trends', ARL Systems and Procedures Exchange Center Flyer 202; available at: *www.webcitation.org/5LrbLKI6Y* (accessed: 13 January 2007).

Pocock, S.J., Hughes, M.D. and Lee, R.J. (1987) 'Statistical problems in the reporting of clinical trials. A survey of three medical journals', *New England Journal of Medicine*, 317: 426–32.

Roiq, M. (2007) 'Avoiding plagiarism, self-plagiarism, and other questionable writing practices: a guide to ethical writing'; available at: *www.webcitation.org/5OC2BmoxS* (accessed: 18 April 2007).

Schafner, A.C. (1994) 'The future of scientific journals: lessons from the past', *Information Technology and Libraries*, 13: 239–47.

Slaughter, J. (2007) *Constitutions and Bylaws*; available at: *www.webcitation.org/5QupbWGaW* (accessed: 7 August 2007).

Solomon, D.J. (2007) 'The role of peer review for scholarly journals in the information age', *Journal of Electronic Publishing*, 10(1); available at: *http://hdl.handle.net/2027/spo.3336451.0010.107* (accessed: 7 August 2007).

Stranack, K. (2006) 'Getting found, staying found, increasing impact. Enhancing readership and preserving content for OJS journals', Public Knowledge Project;

available at: *www.webcitation.org/5P6Vd3kVN* (accessed: 25 May 2007).

Tesdahl, D.B. (2005) *The Nonprofit Board's Guide to Bylaws* (excerpts); available at: *www.webcitation.org/5QurDFW74* (accessed: 7 August 2007).

Van Orsdel, L. and Born, K. (2002) 'Periodicals price survey 2002: doing the digital flip', *Library Journal*, 15 April; available at: *www.webcitation.org/5LrbS6aLk* (accessed: 13 January 2007).

Walsh, N. (2007) 'A technical introduction to XML'; available at: *www.webcitation.org/5QujMB6tE* (accessed: 6 August 2007).

Willinsky, J. (2006) *The Access Principle: The Case for Open Access to Research and Scholarship*. Cambridge, MA: MIT Press; available at: *www.webcitation.org/5QuoLppQ2* (accessed: 7 August 2007).

Willinsky, J. and Wolfson, L. (2001) 'The indexing of scholarly journals: a tipping point for publishing reform?', *Journal of Electronic Publishing*, 7(2); available at: *www.webcitation.org/5LrbVQfcH* (accessed: 13 January 2007).

Websites

American Psychological Association style guide: *www.webcitation.org/5OKGF5KZo*.

AWStats: *www.webcitation.org/5PayTJ0UC*.

Berne Convention: *www.webcitation.org/5NvOefj9u*.

Bruce Clay Inc.: *www.webcitation.org/5PfnOtqQ2*.

Creative Commons: *www.webcitation.org/5NyHV4PZn*.

Directory of Open Access Journals (DOAJ): *www.webcitation.org/5SdGZMgV0*.

Education Policy Analyst Archives: *www.webcitation.org/5Qukfo84y*.

First Monday: *www.firstmonday.org/*.

Google Analytics: *www.webcitation.org/5Pb0N0bDz*.

HTML Document Structure: *www.webcitation.org/5PWH PRuTK*.

Information Research: *http://informationr.net/ir/index.html*.

IR template: *www.webcitation.org/5Q9juGEVZ*.

ISSN Centre Search: *www.webcitation.org/5Pgj3o8WZ*.

Journal of Electronic Publishing: *www.hti.umich.edu/j/jep/*.

Journal of Medical Internet Research: *www.webcitation.org/ 5NwssREcf*.

LOCKSS: *www.lockss.org/lockss/Home*.

Medical Education Online: *www.med-ed-online.org*.

OAIster: *www.oaister.org/*.

Open Archives Initiative Protocol for Metadata Harvesting: *www.webcitation.org/5PK1UEHnz*.

Open Directory Project (ODP): *www.webcitation.org/ 5PRiC89eb*.

Open Journal System (OJS): *www.webcitation.org/5MvFe7h3e*.

Open Society Institute: *www.webcitation.org/5OmRYAx2h*.

Public Knowledge Project (PKP): *www.webcitation.org/ 5MvErB1Hy*.

Scholarly Exchange: *www.webcitation.org/5QupAAhL5*.

Scientific Electronic Library Online (SciELO): *www.web citation.org/5P3BP4aXp*.

SearchEngineWatch.com: *www.webcitation.org/5PXV1t22c*.

SEMPRO: *www.webcitation.org/5PWP3AQYz*.

SPARC publishing resources page: *www.webcitation.org/ 5Mx98xweh*.

Universal Copyright Convention: *www.webcitation.org/ 5NvOsYZY9*.

Webalizer: *www.webcitation.org/5Pac3GNkz*.

WebCite consortium: *www.webcitation.org*.

Index

CPSIA information can be obtained
at www.ICGtesting.com
Printed in the USA
FFOW01n1137180315
11954FF